The Source for Brain-Based Learning

Clare B. Jones

LinguiSystems

LinguiSystems, Inc.
3100 4th Avenue
East Moline, IL 61244-9700

1-800-PRO IDEA
1-800-776-4332

FAX: 1-800-577-4555
E-mail: service@linguisystems.com
Web: www.linguisystems.com

TDD: 1-800-933-8331
(for those with hearing impairments)

Skills:	General Language
Ages:	5-16
Grades:	K-11

Printed in the U.S.A.
ISBN 0-7606-0462-2

About the Author

Clare B. Jones, Ph.D., is a nationally-recognized author, diagnostic specialist, presenter, and trainer. Dr. Jones is the former director of education for Phoenix Children's Hospital and Director of Special Education for the Lakewood City Schools. She was also a classroom teacher for over twenty years. Dr. Jones has received the Hall of Fame Award from CHADD (Children and Adults with Attention Deficit Disorders) in 2001 and was honored as a Master Teacher in Ohio by the Martha Holden Jennings Foundation. She has received numerous awards and honors, including California Community Educator of the year and Visiting Instructor of the Year at Cleveland State University. She has taught classes at Cleveland State University, Arizona State University, Northern Arizona University, and Glendale Community College. Dr. Jones is the author of five books and numerous articles. She is currently on the editorial advisory staff of *Attention* magazine and writes a bimonthly column for *ADDitude* magazine on the Internet. She is married, a mother, and lives in Scottsdale, Arizona, where she maintains a practice, Developmental Learning Associates, L.L.C., and often writes from her second home in Santa Fe, New Mexico. *The Source for Brain-Based Learning* is Clare's first publication with Linguisystems.

Dedication

This book is dedicated to the thousands of teachers who have contacted me over the years, read my books, attended my workshops and offered me advice and warm thoughts. You are my colleagues, my partners, and my friends in the world of education. Thank you for your inspiration and enthusiastic support. I am ever grateful.

Table of Contents

In the summer of 2000 LinguiSystems held its annual National Language Conference on a cruise ship in the Caribbean. I was fortunate enough to be one of the speakers at that conference and was also able to enjoy the cruise with my family. During an opportunity to speak with the LinguiSystems staff, several members brought up the idea of my writing a book for their company. I was honored and began to think of my personal interests and newly developing interests. Brain-based learning seemed a natural progression for my work, and this book is the result of that beginning exploration and an idea that took seed somewhere in the Eastern Caribbean.

Many experts have conducted studies and written in the areas of brain development and brain-based learning. I am indebted to the teachings of David A. Sousa, Marilee B. Sprenger, John Ratey, Eric Jensen, the Caines, and others who inspired me to learn from their work and research. As I immersed myself in the literature, I began to see a correlation between what we identify as brain-based strategies and exemplary teaching. I am pleased that my own natural instincts and soul as a teacher seemed to guide me on the right path. I hope you will find the same experience as you journey through this book.

Clare

> Everyone has inside of him a piece of good news. The good news is that you don't know how great you can be! How much you can love! What you can accomplish! And what your potential is!
> —Anne Frank

1   Brain Research

The field of education has always been subject to the whims of society. During the time of Sputnik, the public's awareness turned to science issues. Teachers were urged to integrate more math and science curricula to support the children of the next generation. Likewise, when the country's population began to increase in the amount of Latino and Mexican immigrants, educators were urged to get up-to-date and be trained in bilingual education. More recently, as society began to accept the field of computer technology and Internet communication, educators were urged to become computer savvy in order to bring their young charges into the millennium with the ability to be proficient in computers and communication technology. Over the years, education has been able to respond to the needs of the people it serves.

Today, brain research has evolved rapidly beyond simply *speculating* about possible trends, to truly *understanding* that this new information has a huge impact on why we think the way we do. Educators will need to respond to this growing amount of research because it is the design for the future.

President George Bush's 1990 proclamation labeling the 1990s as the "Decade of the Brain" brought public awareness to the benefits to be derived from brain research. It also stimulated funds for research in many fields and the notion that there should be a mutual sharing of ideas. Now, in the new millennium, this initial research is beginning to bear fruit. Coming years promise to yield rapid new information about how the brain develops and how children's capacities grow and mature. Advances in genetic studies, neuroscience, and the use of incredible brain imaging machines to aid the search have opened a real window into the mind's patterns and functions. New information about genetic mapping and further insight into the neurochemistry of the brain show us the likelihood that the next generation of teachers will have more information about learning than ever before. The advanced study of the brain and the impact that this new research will have on our understanding should eventually help us to create truly individualized instruction.

Here is a glimpse into the future — can you imagine this scenario? An educator or therapist puts a child's name into a computer and receives immediate information regarding exactly how that child learns, remembers, and processes new information. There will be no more guessing to determine if a child is perhaps an auditory or a visual learner: with this new information you won't have to wonder. The specific details will be provided and you will apply or chart what type of learning activities will be most successful for this student.

Future generations of educators will have incredible biological information at their fingertips, that when linked to common teaching practice will change the learning process. Information from this new field of brain research will allow us to unlock learning and pinpoint exact learning experiences.

Responding to New Information About the Brain

Are we as a culture wise enough and perceptive enough about children to respond to new information about the brain's workings with a positive and proactive reaction? Can we ethically accept this responsibility? Will this research make **genetic swapping** and **cloning** the buzzwords of future developing populations? What will the implications be if this information falls into the *wrong* hands? Preconceived limits of what a child can and cannot learn based on scientific explanations may negatively impact children and will limit the good that this information can accomplish. One can only hope that this information will be handled with respect and sound planning. The test of a responsible society will lie in how it will use the information from the field of neuroscience to improve itself.

Research leaders in all fields — education, psychology, media, government, science, and law — will need to pool their resources and devise a policy of how our nation will respond to this new information. Together as a community, we will want to develop responsible principles and practices in response to this emerging field of brain research. As educators, we are the perfect professionals to utilize this research and bring it into the mainstream. We can correlate what we know about good teaching practice and apply it to the evolving theories about the brain. We will want to mobilize efforts on behalf of the children we serve to help society benefit from the practical parts of this information.

A joint conference convened by the Families and Work Institute in 1997 presented its impression of the acquired knowledge about early brain development in the report "Rethinking the Brain." Their documentation stated the following:

1. An individual's capacity to learn and thrive in a variety of settings depends on the interplay between nature (his genetic endowment) and nurture (the kind of care, stimulation, and teaching he receives).

2. The human brain, across all ethnic and racial groups, is uniquely constructed to benefit from experience and from good teaching, particularly during the first years of life.

3. While the opportunities and risks are greatest during the first years of life, we cannot lose sight that learning takes place throughout the human life cycle (Shore, 1997, p. 4).

"Your Mission, Should You Choose to Accept It . . ."

Educators can best respond to the new directions in brain research by seeing themselves as environmental engineers. An environmental engineer arranges the learning environment for the child's success and encourages learning through that environment (Jones, 1998). We must recognize that we are only a *part* of the learning environment not *all* of it. The teacher offers opportunities for children to maximize their learning and begin to develop adaptive and independent living behaviors. The environmental educator offers the opportunity for the child to develop to the best of his or her ability within an environment that is based on a student's own unique strengths and learning opportunities.

Hot Off the Press!

An incredible amount of new research and scientific information on the brain is being shared almost daily. The purpose of this book is to review that data and share it with professionals who are beginning on the path of integrating this new information into their lesson plans and therapy sessions. It will allow you as the educator to put your own stamp on the data and to be able to continue to make changes in the way you serve children, thus providing the support that you deem necessary. This book in no way is a definitive answer but rather a compilation of ideas, interventions, and strategies based on what we *currently* know about the brain.

> ". . . new research and scientific information on the brain is being shared almost daily."

We begin our journey by starting with the most basic information about the brain that will help us develop our own teaching and learning strategies. In Chapter 2 we will learn that there are certain basic beliefs about the brain that need to be understood before we can conceptualize learning outcomes and interventions. This book can provide a first step for you as you move forward with and ahead of the field using this new *information of the future*! In the words of Abraham Lincoln, "If we could first know where we are, and what we are tending, we could better judge what to do and how to do it."

The Tool Box

The new information available to us today about the brain is the product of state-of-the-art scientific instruments that allow us to actually observe the brain and how it functions.

It will be helpful for you to first know briefly what tools researchers are using to interpret how the brain functions. The machines that are making a difference include the following:

- **Ultrasound:** This imaging technology analyzes how sound waves bounce off internal body parts and then translates this information into a computerized image. Some of us have already had experience with this technology as expectant parents observing the ultrasound pictures of an unborn infant.

- **Computerized Tomography Scan (CT or CAT):** This uses focused X-Rays to produce detailed cross-sections of the brain structure. It can detect strokes, cancer, and malformations or injury to the brain, but it cannot detect actual function.

- **Magnetic Resonance Imaging Scan (MRI):** This technology produces detailed images of any internal body part. It works by exposing the body to a magnetic field (radio waves) and measuring the energy, called **nuclear magnetic resonance**, that bounces off atoms within the body. The computer then translates this data into a detailed image. It can take a picture of the brain once every second and show us the brain's structure and function. A related technology called **Functional MRI** offers insight into how various parts of the body, including specific regions of the brain, work or do not work. It reveals brain activity by measuring blood flow and provides information about the changes in the blood from volume to flow to oxygenation, which occur when the body undertakes various tasks. A Functional MRI can observe both motor tasks, such as a handshake or eating an apple, to cognitive tasks, such as solving a problem.

- **Positron Emission Tomography (PET) Scan:** This machine shows how the brain works. It actually demonstrates how the brain uses energy. To perform a PET scan, scientists inject a subject with a tracer chemical. This chemical compound contains an isotope that emits particles called **positrons**. This compound closely resembles glucose, the brain's chief energy source. Thus, the brain is tricked into taking up the tracer chemical and trying to use it to fuel its various activities. By using a special camera, scientists can then look at the images the PET scan creates and see how different parts of the brain use the injected material. The result is a picture on a computer screen in color demonstrating your brain in action that helps scientists analyze the brain's functions.

- **Electroencephalogram (EEG):** The EEG detects and records brain waves. It allows us to see how the brain reacts to various environmental factors, such as stress and comforting care. It actually measures the following four types of brain waves
  - ✔ *beta:* alert wakefulness
  - ✔ *alpha:* relaxed wakefulness
  - ✔ *theta:* the onset of sleep
  - ✔ *delta:* deep sleep

- **Magneto encephalography (MEG):** This is a more sophisticated form of the EEG, which can actually yield 4,000 magnetic brain measurements per second. It is more than twice as fast as the EEG.

- **Single Photon Emission Computerized Tomography (SPECT):** This is an imaging system that gives a close approximation of dopamine activity in the brain. It detects a tag attached to the dopamine transporter and allows scientists to follow the activity around the brain.

Point of Interest

Each research instrument listed, although technical in nature, has its own mnemonic symbol after its name (PET, EEG, etc.). Scientists frequently use mnemonics to aid in recall of complicated terms. Scientists recognize that mnemonics offer a "shorthand" technique for remembering information. The mnemonics used for the instruments are called **acronyms**. Acronyms use the first letter of each word to make a shorter word, which is easier to memorize. Acronyms are helpful when we need to remember more complicated material. We use these acronyms to trigger our brain's memory pathways. Thus, as we introduce new vocabulary, it is often helpful to use acronyms to help us remember information we want to recall later. We will learn later in this book why these mnemonics work and can be excellent teaching tools for students of any age!

Meet the Brain

Have you ever given much thought to what your brain actually looks like?

If you imagine your brain to be one big neutral colored mass of bumpy matter, you are partially correct. It is light gray to brownish and is jelly-like in substance. Each section of the brain, however, has its own unique mission and function, so the brain is really more defined and detailed than the term "jelly-like" would connote.

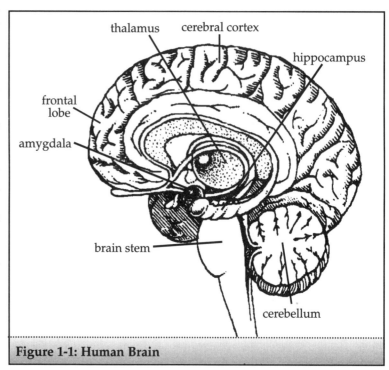

Figure 1-1: Human Brain

First, understand that the brain is divided into two **hemispheres**: right and left. For some reason, we have yet to understand, the nerves from the left side of the body cross over to the right hemisphere and the nerves of the right cross to the left! These two hemispheres each have their own four **lobes**. A thin, tough laminated cortex covers the hemispheres, which is roughly 1/10th of an inch thick. Each one of eight lobes has countless folds or **fissures**. They actually look something like waves or wrinkles. These folds appear to mature at different times in a person's life span, and it is interesting to note that some of these folds are not even developed at birth. The chemicals in your brain foster development of the fissures, and depending upon when these chemicals send out messages, there are specific time frames when certain kinds of learning occur. These time frames are real and they are observed by all of us in the developmental pattern of normal growth. The time frames when certain learning experiences occur are why we, for example, do not expect a baby who is starting to talk to be able to count immediately also, but we do expect the child to be able to count when they are old enough to start kindergarten.

Meet the Cerebral Cortex

Now that you can envision the brain and its folds, let's explore where the majority of the brain's work really occurs. If we were able to peel back the skin and actually look inside the brain and investigate its layers, the first layer we would see would be the **cerebral cortex**. The cerebral cortex is the upper ridged part of the brain that contains the two main hemispheres. Most of what we call "brain work" actually occurs here. Thinking, planning, and remembering are handled by the cerebral cortex. The front of the cerebrum is called the **frontal lobe** or **frontal cortex**. The frontal lobe is considered the executive center of the brain. It is sort of like the "CEO" of the brain. It is the part of your brain where your emotions are regulated, where your problem-solving capacity exists, and is the location of most of your working memory. The frontal lobe is responsible for the executive functions of initiating and sustaining activities, prioritizing, strategizing, and most importantly, inhibiting impulses until the brain can rationally weigh possible consequences of the activity (Giedd, 2000). Research indicates that the frontal lobe is particularly slow at maturing. As a result, its folds develop slowly. Most researchers concur that the frontal lobe does not develop until full maturation and it is still developing during adolescence. Therefore, one can assume that because the frontal lobe is slower to develop, the full emotional regulation capability of the frontal lobe is not totally operational until later in life. Many believe that this lag in growth contributes to the slow development of emotional maturity. David Sousa, a leading author in brain research comments, "Because the rational system matures slowly in adolescents, they are more likely to submit to their emotions" (Sousa, 2001).

> "The frontal lobe is considered the executive center of the brain. It is sort of like the 'CEO' of the brain."

Also located in the cerebral cortex is the area where the short-term (immediate) memory is stored. In 1998, researchers at the National Institute of Mental Health, (NIMH) a component of the National Institutes of Health, pinpointed the short-term memory section of the cerebral cortex, stating that it is specifically just above the right eye in the right hemisphere, in the right frontal lobe area. They feel this is the part of the brain that momentarily holds information about the location of items. As you will see, information about what the different sections of the brain are responsible for can allow us to understand certain steps in development more readily.

Looking Further at the Lobes

The **temporal lobes** are located above the ears, which appear to deal with sound, speech, and some aspects of long-term memory. Moving toward the back of the brain, we find the occipital lobe, and like its name portrays, it is the area of the brain used for visual processing. Located directly on top of the brain is the parietal lobe, which appears to deal with calculation and orientation. This is the section of the left side of the brain where mathematics learning literally occurs. Next time you are working on your income tax, rub this part of your brain for support!

Stretching between the frontal lobes and the parietal lobe is a band, which actually reaches from ear to ear, called the **motor cortex**. Visualize it as a rubber band, because in the same simple way a rubber band controls loose papers, it controls your body movement. The motor cortex works within the cerebellum to help you coordinate your motor skills.

The Control Center

The **brain stem,** upon which the cerebral cortex "rests," is considered the core and oldest part of the brain. Researchers, who study evolution and the first Neanderthal man believed it evolved 500 million years ago. The brain stem is the vital control section of the brain where the heartbeat, body temperature, digestion, and respiration are monitored. The brain stem houses the brain's reticular activating system (RAS), which is in charge of the brain's alertness.

Beyond the Brain stem

As we move above the brain stem, we see the **thalamus**, **hippocampus**, and the **amygdala**. These parts of the brain play a role in sensory information storage and reaction. These structures make up the **limbic center** of the brain. The thalamus is the receptor for environmental sensory stimulus that enter the brain. The thalamus receives vision and taste stimuli, but not smell. When it receives the sensory information, it sends it to other parts of the brain for continued processing.

The hippocampus is the storage center in your brain. Within its depths you will find such things as the memory of your grandmother's face and the details of your first date. The hippocampus plays a large role in learning, as its responsibility is to constantly check information relayed to the working memory and compare it to stored experiences. Some musicians and writers refer to this as the mind's "attic." Without these permanent memories, there is no reason for creating associations or assigning meaning to experiences. The hippocampus performs the critical action of creating meaning from our thoughts. The hippocampus is the region of the brain most sensitive to stress (Jacobs and Nadel, 1985). Together, the hippocampus and amygdala, as well as other parts of the brain, (remember these things all work together as a great team) are important to reacting to stress and controlling emotions.

Some researchers feel the amygdala is actually the specific structure in the brain *most* responsible for emotions, stress, and fear. (The next time you are stressed out, blame it on <u>Amy</u> in your <u>amygdala</u>!) There is also research linking this emotion center of the brain to our long-term memory. The hypothesis is that an emotional link to long-term memory is possible because our emotions seem so triggered by built-up exposure and experiences. This creates the speculation that thoughts, which stay in the long-term memory, may be connected with emotional experiences of all types. We will investigate more about this emotional connection in later chapters.

Further Scientific Support
We now move from examining the main structures of the brain to describing "activity central," or the messengers responsible for activity within the brain.

Along with the various scientific instruments that help us study the actual scope of the brain and its structure and shape, a group of researchers are also studying the chemical makeup of the brain. Researchers are interested in finding out how these chemicals relate to specific functions. They are further exploring what can happen if these chemicals are altered in some way, either due to injury or intake of various substances such as nicotine and methamphetimine. Scientists call these areas of the brain **neurotransmitters**, or segments, of the brain. As the "message makers" in the brain, their job is to transmit and make sense out of the billions of messages the brain receives.

To better understand these message makers of the brain some further explanation of terms is necessary:

✔ **Neurotransmitters:** These are the chemical substances that transmit impulses in the brain from neuron to neuron across the synaptic gap. There are approximately 100 chemicals stored in axon sacs in the brain. Two of these substances are serotonin and dopamine. They act like the "directors" of the neurons.

✔ **Neuron:** This is one of the two cells that are part of the brain and central nervous system. Within each neuron lies an axon, a cell body, and numerous dendrites. Dendrites are like small hairs and actually receive incoming signals from another neuron.

As we age, the number of neurons remains stable but they grow in both size and mass. It is estimated at birth that an infant has 100 billion brain cells. A single cell can team with and connect with as many as 15,000 other cells. A **synapse** is produced when the axon of one neuron connects with the dendrite of another. In brief, they connect, and a synapse is created. Each neuron can make more than 10,000 synapses. There is a significant difference in the rate at which this can happen. Synapses are created in children's brains at twice the rate of the synapses in an adult brain.

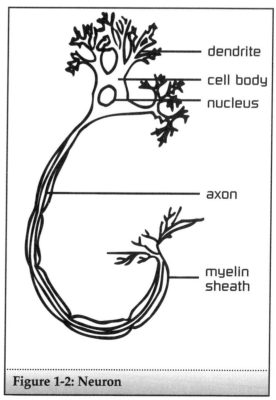

Figure 1-2: Neuron

Thus, the child can learn twice as fast when introduced to new material. One of the most significant reasons why we want to create quality educational experiences for young children is that during the first decade of life, their brains are two and a half times more active than at any other time in their existence.

✔ **Glial Cells:** The brain contains two main types of cells — neurons, as mentioned above, and glial cells. Glial cells support and complement the various functions of neurons. Think of them as the support team. They are like the cheerleaders in the brain. During brain development these glial cells form long chains, often called "cortical ladders," over which the neurons travel or climb to reach their proper position. This is called **cortical cell migration** or **neuronal migration**.

✔ **Cortical Neuron:** This is the name for the specific brain cell that is in the cerebral cortex. The cerebral cortex is the outer portion of the cerebrum. It is filled with these neurons.

Connections Matter!

All of the brain cells send out signals to one another and receive input from other cells. Neurotransmitters such as dopamine and serotonin travel quickly and make new connections. The signals they send are actually electrical impulses. As we activate networks of neurons, they strengthen their connections. These message makers are the brain's "wiring."

At age three your network of connections is dense, with approximately one thousand trillion connections. This network does not continue to get thicker and thicker, nor does it remain stable. Instead, somewhere around age eleven, your brain will slowly begin to get rid of superfluous connections (ones you don't need)

> ". . . somewhere around age eleven, your brain will slowly get rid of superfluous connections (ones you don't need) and end up with a sparkling, well-designed and smoothly functioning brain network."

and end up with a sparkling, well-designed and smoothly functioning brain network. By the time you reach adulthood, your brain connections are efficient, powerful, and now permanent. The brain will discard any connection that is not used. The old adage, "use it or lose it" certainly applies here. This process of casting off unnecessary connections helps us understand why a skill that has not "connected" at an early age, will not be acquired as the child ages. For example, imagine a child who has had limited experiences with play and social interaction. The child may have been isolated from all normal social contact and was rarely played with in the early years. This child may have severe difficulty mastering appropriate social skills and his or her personal social development will be markedly delayed. Here's another example: visualize a child who has not heard a single spoken word by age ten. The loss of connections that this child has experienced indicates he or she will never adequately learn a language. The part of the brain responsible for language connections never developed and the connections were eliminated. If the child hears language at age ten for the first time, the brain will not know what to do with the sound and certainly cannot imitate it. The section of the brain that was to have developed to carry on this task did not, and it is unable to make a connection. Neuroscience has shown us that there is a period of time in development when the brain is ready to receive certain types of information. If, however, the information is not forthcoming, the brain may never be able to receive it. This phenomena occurs not only in the world of the human species but in the animal kingdom as well. The great horned owl is a skilled hunter known for swiftly grasping its prey once it has recognized its movement. If a baby great horned owl is taken from its mother and does not have the opportunity to learn to hunt — a skill it learns as a developing bird — then he will never learn to hunt.

Review Time

The sequence of the way the brain develops appears to be programmed genetically right from the start of the developing embryo. State-of-the-art instruments allow us to study the step-by-step process in a developing brain.

1. The **brain stem** develops first biologically. It has the responsibility of controlling basic bodily functions like temperature, heartbeat, and respiration.

2. The **cerebellum** and **basal ganglia** are next to appear. They are programmed to control movement.

3. The **limbic system** (thalamus, hippocampus, etc.) develops next, supporting emotion and memory.

4. The last system to develop is the **cerebral cortex**. Gradual maturation and logical higher-order thinking are the primary functions of this section.

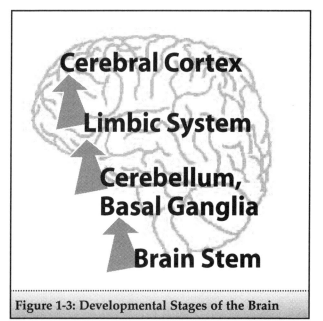

Figure 1-3: Developmental Stages of the Brain

Team Thought

From the frontal lobes on the cerebrum to deep inside the brain where the neurons exist, no one part of the brain works in isolation. The segments are all in network or tandem with one another. All areas of the brain synchronize thoughts together in a very complex network; therefore, true "brain work" is the actual result of the brain's action and literally a result of teamwork, also known as **team thought**. All parts of the brain work together for action, planning, memory, and thought. We have learned that should just one part of the brain fail to respond in its normal pattern (i.e., let down the team), then a part of that type of learning may be closed permanently to the brain.

Some researchers refer to periods of time when the brain is most receptive to learning (synchronizing its activities) as a "window of opportunity." others refer to it as a "critical period" or "plastic stages." Today, as we study developmental patterns of learning, brain research is helping us see why such a period of opportunity is so critical in the development of the mind. This new research is allowing us to see that different stages of learning are most functional during specific times of our life. It behooves us as educators to know when these general opportunities of time are available. Once we are aware of these limitations on the time a skill has to develop, we can maximize specific learning strategies. It is most likely that if you expand and learn a skill at the opportune time in development, you will really master the skill. Does this mean if you miss this chance you can never achieve some level of learning? The fact that a learning opportunity has passed by does not entirely limit the person from developing that area, but it does restrict the level to which the skill will be acquired. For example, if you miss one time frame for which math and logic skills are best learned, you may still be able to develop an ability for it later in life. The price you pay, however is that you will work a lot harder to obtain the skill and maintain it. Also, the level at which you are able to use that skill will not be as high if you had started developing it at the correct developmental time.

> "It is most likely that if you expand and learn a skill at the opportune time in development, you will really master the skill."

Can these specific time limitations be changed or refigured to open opportunities for learning later? Some scientists are indeed seeking to determine if we can rejuvenate a part of the brain that has not developed to its full capacity for learning. They would like to use electronic devices and other types of new technology, including lasers, to see if we can reconstruct these lost developmental pathways in the brain in much the same way we rescue files when our computer's hard drive has crashed. When we see how far technology has come over the past decade, we can only wonder if someday, someone will create a way to salvage a lost neural connection and re-establish it. Only time will tell. Meanwhile, the good news is this: Once something is learned, it

is retained equally well by all age groups, even if it takes a bit longer for an older person to learn it (Patoine, 2001).

What's Next?

In summary, substantial progress has been and continues to be made in our understanding of the functions of the brain. High-quality assessments and treatments continue to develop and will be a realistic part of the future. New studies will continually astonish us and for many it will be a waiting process. However, in the meantime, educators can begin to work at improving the current educational system for children with the information we do have.

2 Critical and Sensitive Periods of Learning

What is the difference between a world-class instrumentalist and someone who began learning the instrument at the age of 18? The world-class maestro undoubtedly began training on the instrument as a toddler. Mozart was composing and playing music at age four. His parents were musicians and he was exposed to music from conception. Bobby Fisher, international chess master, played chess matches as a preschooler. Almost all world-class musicians and chess players began their training at a very early age. This often explains their competence. Their success is not based on the amount of time they spend practicing but how intuitively they understand the process of the act itself. They were learning music or chess at *the* critical period of development when their rapidly growing brain was able to make the type of neural connections needed to link patterns into their very nature of thinking. This makes music or chess for them as automatic as sleeping, walking, or riding a bicycle. Compare other world-class competitors in different athletic fields such as golf, ice-skating, and swimming. The most successful ones began to develop their talents at an age where developmentally this instruction made the learning experience almost automatic.

Not long ago, neuroscientists speculated that the brain actually stopped growing by the time a child was five years old. By then, it was thought, nearly all of the brain's synapses had been connected and the only remaining task for the brain was to program those connections. Now researchers have detected brain growth throughout childhood and well into adolescence in certain areas. There are, however, as we stated before, suggested areas of time when cognitive functioning will be at its utmost and opportune time to receive stimulus. In neurobiological literature, these periods of time are often referred to as "critical periods," "windows of opportunity," or "plastic periods." I will refer to them as "prime time" periods. In

"Now researchers have detected brain growth throughout childhood and well into adolescence in certain areas."

general, those periods signify a span of time in the developmental process when major modifications in the brain's formation appear to be possible. These are the optimum times of development during which the brain is particularly proficient at explicit types of learning. In the book, *Rethinking the Brain*, researcher Harry Chugani is quoted as saying, "This is the opportunity, for us to be able to use the environmental exposure to change the anatomy of the brain and make it more efficient." He, along with other researchers, suggests that familiarity and practice during the prime times create opportunities for continuing certain kinds of neural pathways. Learning can develop at any time during a lifespan, but it is during these prime times that the brain will experience the maximum in cognitive return. In this way, experience plays a crucial role in "wiring" a young child's brain (Shore, 1997).

Prime Time Intervals

Here is an overview of suggested critical periods — the prime time where researchers have detected brain growth at its peak. The following pages show how prime time growth relates to vision, hearing, emotion, vocabulary, language, math/logic, and gross and fine motor development.

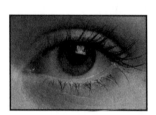

Vision

During an infant's first minute of life, the brain is responding to visual images as the child opens his or her eyes to new visual stimulation. Research indicates that if the brain does not receive any visual stimuli by age two, a person will never have typically normal vision. (This finding does not take into account a retina transplant or surgical restoration of vision.) Thus, the ages of zero to ten years are the prime times for providing visual stimulation and visual processing. Meltzoff, Gopnik, and Kuhl (1999) note that 40 minutes after birth babies can imitate facial expressions. They note that from the start, babies see faces and know they are like other people.

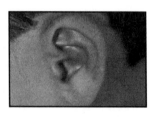

Hearing

If a person is born profoundly deaf and does not hear any word or sound until age ten, that person will never learn a language. However, if a person is given the opportunity to hear for the first time at age ten, perhaps through an organ implant or some other type of technology, they may be able to learn language. It will, however, take considerable effort and time to develop at least rudimentary language skills.

Motor Development

Gross and fine motor skills develop between the ages of zero and eight years. As with any age group, not all children fit these average patterns or demonstrate all of the abilities, but the majority of motor skills do develop during these periods.

If given the opportunity to highly specialize during these years (learning golf, for example) the child will undoubtedly develop higher-level motor skills in these specified areas. Tiger Woods, a highly recognized professional golfer, was using a putter skillfully by age three. "Research confirms that the young brain is fully ready to learn through tactile 'touch' by nine months of age" (Sousa, 2001).

For fine motor skill growth, grasp begins at age three months. Pincer grasp (finger and thumb) emerges at around seven to twelve months of age. By nine to twelve months, some infants are able to hold a crayon and to make marks (some can scribble). Good hand and finger coordination is possible by two and one half years to three years. For gross motor skills, at age two a child can kick and catch a large ball, step up on a block and back down, and climb and manage small indoor stairs. At age three, a child can focus on a target in throwing or kicking and will enjoy balls of all sizes. By age five, gross motor skills are well developed and the child should be able to run, jump, climb, and balance. From age five to eight, fine-tuning of basic motor skills occurs.

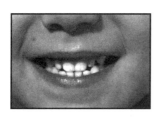

Emotional Control

It is noted that between eight to thirty months the child begins to experience increased metabolic activity in the frontal cortex (the part of the brain that is associated with the ability to regulate and express emotion, as well as to think and plan). The child is beginning to experience self-regulatory control and reaction to emotions. The temperament and style of emotional recovery begins to be established for the child. Somewhere around age eleven, the brain undergoes major reorganization in an area associated with such things as social behavior and impulse control. Activity in the frontal cortex seems particularly active after puberty. (Remember, prior to this time, this area of the cerebrum is not fully developed.) The frontal cortex is where logical decision-making or problem solving occurs, and neuroscientists have determined that this is the area responsible for executive functions. It is highly regulated by emotional response, and it is the last area of the brain to fully develop. Since this area is not fully developed, and basically "under new construction" after the age of eleven, the child moving into adolescence is more likely to have difficulty making decisions *without* some type of an emotional response. Risk-taking, impulsive choices, and reckless behavior may accompany this age span. Does this make it easier for you to understand the roller coaster emotions of a teenager?

Adolescence is a period when the developing brain is most vulnerable to traumatic experiences, drug abuse, and other unhealthy influences (Crenson, 2001). Because the brain structure is not yet fully developed, children at this age may not easily handle higher order thinking patterns. This underdevelopment results in their struggles in handling social pressure, suppressing impulsive desires, and managing other stresses the way more mature adults do. They will typically have difficulty making decisions and selecting their own choices because they are just beginning to learn how to assess the risk level in an activity. This research has helped us understand that the emotional growth of the developing brain is highly responsive to emotions and very reactive to change.

Vocabulary

At three to six months infants can localize sounds, begin to babble, and make singing sounds with an adult. Actual word naming and vocabulary development occurs between eight months to six years. Most children will develop a vocabulary of ten words a day at somewhere around eight to nine months. By age three, they will have a vocabulary of approximately 900 words. This will increase to 2500 to 3000 words by age five. From then on, exposure to increasing vocabulary opportunities will benefit the child in developing ongoing language (Diamond & Hoppson, 1998).

Language Areas

Language understanding, sentence formation, and conversation develops from about eighteen months to twelve years. Researchers Chomsky and Bellugi believe we are all born with an innate capacity to learn a language. They argue that we are not born with any predisposition to speak a particular language, say English, but that through exposure, our brains conform to the structure of the specific language we hear. They indicate that in order to develop a bilingual experience, parents should introduce two languages simultaneously to their children from birth to ten or twelve years. This exposure to dual languages, they believe, will encourage the child to develop bilingual skills more easily than just introducing one language at this time.

Developmental difficulties in speech and language patterns can also be observed at an early age. Language disabilities such as stuttering and phonological disorders will emerge as the child struggles to duplicate sounds. These problems will be most obvious during the critical period of speech development from two-and-one-half to twelve years of age.

Mathematical/Logic Ability

Research indicates that the child is developing a sense of reasoning and appreciation of numbers and patterns as early as five months old. Studies indicate that this rapid absorption of math logic is evident up to age four. These formative first years are where many mathematicians developed their cognition and logic for numbers and concepts because the brain is developing its innate sense for math, logic, and pattern at this time. When fostered, children will intuitively begin to understand grouping, categorization, and estimation. Following this period of early development, we can and do learn specifically the practice and execution of numbers (multiplication, algebra, etc.).

Instrumental Music

Researchers feel the optimum time to expose a child to instrumental music is somewhere between the ages of two and three years and up to age ten. Infants are extraordinarily adept at choosing between well-formed and ill-formed musical sequences in the music of their culture. This early "grammatical" understanding of music's syntax and semantics parallels the child's ability to discern the structural regularities of spoken language. This incredible ability to identify music sequences makes the learning of the instrument far more meaningful and successful at this time (Levitin, 2000, p. 45).

Right Brain/Left Brain

In the first decade of life, a child's brain is formed as he or she experiences the surrounding world and begins to form attachments to parents, family members, and other caregivers. We begin to watch as the child's personality forms, and we see how their interests evolve. We can observe as the child begins to interact with other social beings he or she contacts and we watch as these connections to people seem to matter or not matter. What we are observing in all these activities is a normal pathway as specific sections of the brain mature more rapidly than others. In fact, further studies of the developing brain pattern seem to suggest that at age one children are ready for simple, concrete problem-solving (Hannaford, 1995).

The separate hemispheres of the brain provide different functions of basic problem-solving skills, but the hemispheres do not develop at the same rate. From ages four to seven, the right cerebral hemisphere of the brain is developing more quickly than the left. The branching of the dendrites is dramatically different in the right side than the left side. Here are some characteristics of right brain development from the ages of four to seven:

- The child will form visual images quickly and big picture thinking will evolve.

- Children at this age will respond more impulsively and will function best with more visual stimulation.

- Children will need to be actively involved with their learning experiences; thus, the term "hands-on" brings real meaning to the learning pattern.

From age seven to nine, the left cerebral hemisphere will begin to develop more adequately. Here are some characteristics of left brain development:

- The child will enjoy language stimulation and benefit from the experience of higher-level language skills.

- Girls in particular develop left hemisphere skills more rapidly and will show the development of stronger verbal skills at this time.

- Recall for details and specific ideas regarding pragmatics, structure of language, and syntax will develop.

- Spelling skills emerge, as does the ability to recognize punctuation and capitalization in writing.

- Cognitive (thought) skills are basically still in developmental progress. The child during these ages will need very concrete structured activities with a kinesthetic (hands-on, touch) influence.

At ages eleven through thirteen, the hemispheres should now be fully integrated and the corpus callosum is now mature. The child is now ready for complex abstractions.

In the past, research typically described personalities as more right brained or left brained, but in reality, the hemispheres must work together to develop thought and accomplish complex problem solving. Some people will have had experiences more directed to one area of the brain than another, and they will certainly feel more successful and skilled in that hemisphere than the other. We recognize that a possible explanation for this is that early on they may have had more enriched opportunities to develop skills in one area than another and took advantage of their prime time.

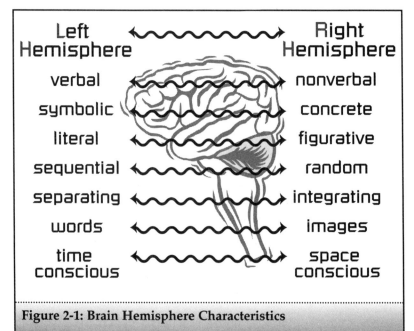

Figure 2-1: Brain Hemisphere Characteristics

An Early Start Is the Best Start

It is evident upon examining the critical periods of brain development that the majority of prime time learning opportunities for vision, hearing, motor, and cognitive growth occur before age eight. Emotional and problem-solving skills appear to be the areas that develop more slowly. Full maturation of higher order response does not often occur until late adolescence or into early adulthood. A newborn child's brain makes connections at earthshaking speed as it absorbs and is stimulated by the environment. Therefore, enriched experiences during the early years of rapid neuron development when the child's brain is reinforcing its wiring is imperative. The richer the environment, the greater the number of interconnections the infant's brain will make. This idea certainly gives substantial support to early intervention, enriched learning environments, and age-appropriate educational programming. In regard to this early period of critical thinking, we must also keep in mind that there are no absolutes. Each human is unique, and we both suspect and observe that children at all ages are at varying levels of brain development.

Additionally, when reviewing a prime time list such as the one provided in Figure 3-2 on page 34, we must keep in mind, that the developmental variability among children is a function of *both* biological and experiential differences. Not all children will fit these average patterns or demonstrate all of these abilities and keen interests. I like to think of prime times as springboards, and just like a diving board, they are the best places to jump off from.

The Influence of Disability

Biological genetic differences and environmental influences can impair certain learning pathways and destroy neuron connections. During pregnancy, the development of the brain is fragile and susceptible to all kinds of disturbance. An injury to the brain during delivery, a loss of oxygen, or toxins such as tobacco, alcohol, or other drugs in the blood system, can all contribute to disrupted brain cell growth and weaker brain development. For example, studies indicate that mothers who smoke more than two packs of cigarettes a day run a high risk of having a child with attention deficit disorder. These external factors influence the formation of networks needed for language or cognitive thought and thus destroy neurons, which eventually lead to learning difficulties.

In addition to outside physical factors, biological tendencies may indicate a genetic link in a family for a disorder resulting in altered brain development. There may be a genetic mutation such as Fragile X or Down's syndrome (extra chromosome) causing a change in the brain's development resulting in a learning deficit. A disability can also be genetically inherited. For example, new research in gene studies (McCracken, 2000) is suggesting an actual genetic link in families with attention disorders. Other researchers (Restak, 2000) have linked prolonged and inappropriate stress in the person's environment as harmful to brain development at any age. Chemicals called **corticosteriods** that are released into the bloodstream during stress can damage the hippocampus and thus interfere with the programming of new information into memory. **Cortisol** alters the brain by making it vulnerable to processes that destroy neurons and reduce the number of synapses in certain parts of the brain. This is the way stressful or traumatic experiences undermine neurological development and impair brain function. We can see that a variety of factors, from biological to environmental can cause disruption and malfunction in brain development.

This information leads us to ponder the following questions about just how influential these prime time periods of development are:

- When these periods are over, is there still a way to impact learning development, or is the area closed permanently?
- Can a person "recover" from the loss of one of these periods?
- Once we are able to obtain knowledge about specific aspects of brain development and functioning, will we be able to design interventions that more closely match children's needs?
- Can we use research to identify a very specific time frame in which to offer interventions so they may do the most good?

These unanswered questions continue to motivate the field of brain research.

What we are aware of is that the brain is able to recover some lost functions, and that this ability is especially remarkable in the first decade of life. Numerous studies show us that the brain can shift functions to different parts of the brain with a resurgence of pathways, allowing a substantial recovery of lost function. A change in environment, increased strategies, and exposure to certain kinds of stimulation in the first decade of life can trigger the brain to regroup and connect in other ways. New connections do occur and that makes learning an ongoing process. What we do develop we can enrich and make even more substantial. In 1997, a research study published in *Nature* showed that an enriched environment might actually increase the number of neurons in the brains of not just infants, but also young adults. We can draw strength in knowing that with more information we will learn many ways to educate and encourage learning opportunities for developing children. Our new insights into brain development will allow us to foster and continue ongoing interest in our children's lives, which will in turn only enrich and better their world.

> "... the brain is able to recover some lost functions, and this ability is especially remarkable in the first decade of life."

Want to Raise Baby's IQ?

✔ Start talking to baby at birth. Increase communication activities between 12 and 18 months of age when the temporal lobe is very receptive (Kotulak, 1996).

✔ Introduce music — listening, making music, and experiences with instruments before age four (Rauscher et al., 1997).

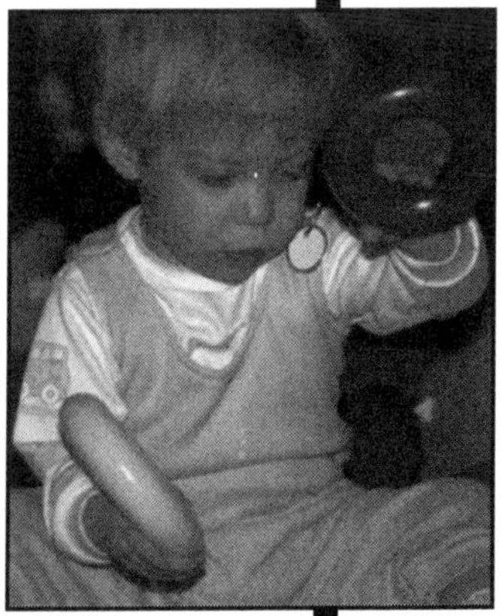

✔ Introduce manipulative and counting games as well as number songs. Infants as young as five months have number sense and reasoning ability for math (Wynn, 1995).

✔ Provide an enriched home environment. Offer opportunities for listening, creating, touching, experiencing, and sharing. Expose the child to a variety of activities based on sensory development and the opportunity to explore the surroundings. Let toddlers satisfy their curiosity and engage in more active play.

✔ Select preschool settings that offer a developmentally-appropriate curriculum (Weikart, 1997).

✔ Introduce a foreign language simultaneously with the child's native language (Diamond & Hopson, 1998).

Figure 2-2: Developmental Tips

> Before I can teach you,
> I must know *how* you learn.
>
> —Clare B. Jones

3 Getting to Know Your Brain

A classroom teacher enters his or her environment in September with a packet of information containing children's names, addresses, ages, and perhaps little else. From this information, and the teacher's experience or training, the entire year's curriculum must be planned. To be fully effective, curriculum should be based on sound theoretical principles of how children develop and learn, but it must also be derived from the needs and interests of individual children. New information on brain research and prime time learning situations provide an additional useful tool for understanding what our curriculum should include. As a result, curriculum development should take into account the following:

1. prime times of learning
2. the knowledge of normal child development stages
3. the individual characteristics of children
4. relevant information about the children's family backgrounds and cultures
5. the values of our society
6. parental concerns
7. knowledge of what children at each age need to know in order to function competently at their grade level

The inclusion of brain research information into curriculum allows us to truly include developmental experiences that enhance a child's optimum learning opportunity at the appropriate level for which it is intended.

Multiple Intelligence Theory

Howard Gardner, the extraordinary professor from Harvard University, helped us see a link in learning styles and environment when he developed his theory of multiple intelligences. In his work through the Project Zero program at Harvard, working in 1985 and

1998, Gardner introduced the theory of multiple intelligences. Gardner notes eight possible ways of expressing one's intelligence.

Here are the eight areas of intelligence Gardner recognized:

1. *Verbal/Linguistic*

   These are the word makers. The groups of people who fall in this category are skilled with thinking and expressing themselves with words. They verbally create pictures and stories for us. They have an average to above average vocabulary and tend to enjoy describing and sharing verbally with their colleagues.

   Famous example — Oprah Winfrey
   Everyday example — teacher

Gardner's 8 Intelligences
1. Verbal/Linguistic
2. Logical/Mathematical
3. Musical/Rhythmic
4. Visual/Spatial
5. Bodily/Kinesthetic
6. Interpersonal
7. Intrapersonal
8. Naturalist

Figure 3-1: Multiple Intelligences

2. *Logical/Mathematical*

   This category includes people who have a natural skill with numbers and logic. They enjoy detail and seek precise and accurate information. They are considered problem solvers.

   Famous example — Charles Schwab
   Everyday example — banker

3. *Musical/Rhythmic*

   Sensitive of sound, this group of people enjoys music, rhythm, and pattern. They sing, hum, and tap out patterns as they sit.

   Famous example — Quincy Jones
   Everyday example — music teacher

4. *Visual/Spatial*

   These people are keenly aware of shapes in space and visual dimension of objects. They like to do puzzles, draw, doodle, and can tell you just where to move your desk when you are planning a room.

   Famous example — Frank Lloyd Wright
   Everyday example — interior designer

5. *Bodily/Kinesthetic*

   Supreme motor awareness and good gross motor skills characterize those who possess this form of intelligence. They are well-organized, planned, and coordinated in both gross and fine motor movements.

   Famous example — Michael Jordan

   Everyday example — aerobics instructor

6. *Interpersonal*

   This might be described as "the thinking man's intelligence." This category is for people who are sensitive to the feelings and needs of others. They interact well with people and are sought out by others to participate on teams or offer advice.

   Famous example — Dr. Joyce Brothers

   Everyday example — therapist/psychologist

7. *Intrapersonal*

   This is also an emotionally-centered form of intelligence. This area applies to deep thinkers who seek introspection, thought, and observation as they work. Often inspirational, they exhibit philosophical interpretations of daily life.

   Famous example — Henry Thoreau

   Everyday example — novelist

8. *Naturalist*

   These groups of people enjoy animals, nature, and plants. They are drawn to the outdoors. They enjoy categorizing and classifying information.

   Famous example — Charles Darwin

   Everyday example — veterinarians

A person can be a combination or blend of several of these intelligences. For example, you can be verbally linguistic and also interpersonal. You can be logical/mathematical and a naturalist. The joy of Gardner's work is that he illustrates that these are the ways we are intelligent and that we can become highly skilled, if not gifted, in these areas if we develop ourselves in nontraditional categories. In his work about unique brains, including the child with ADD/ADHD, Thomas Armstrong refers to these eight areas with a more common jargon approach. He identifies them as the following (Armstrong, 1994):

1. word smart
2. number smart
3. picture smart
4. music smart
5. body smart
6. people smart
7. self smart
8. nature smart

As exciting as all this information has been, it is now apparent in neuroscience research that these eight areas are just the tip of the iceberg and that there are really numerous ways the brain can link these areas of intelligence. There are probably millions of different levels of intelligence. The purpose of studying the multiple intelligence (MI) models is to help us understand that every mind can have these facets; therefore, this theory guides us to perceive our students and colleagues with a healthy regard for their individual strengths.

As an educator, Gardner's work was introduced in the early 1980s (1983) before the recent age of more evolving brain science. He certainly was on the cusp of what was to occur in the educational interpretation of learning, and his work stimulated educators to see more than one side of the story.

Planning Curriculum to Incorporate Brain Research

When you rethink your plan for your classroom curriculum to include brain research information, it is helpful to follow these three guidelines:

1. Get to know your students' preferred modes of learning.

2. Be sensitive to their areas of specific intelligence.

3. Attempt to offer a plan that incorporates all modalities and factors in their learning.

As an educator, I find that this information gives me a more thorough perception of how to plan my curriculum and gives me direction to begin to enhance all students' learning processes.

Suspected Prime Times for Learning

Reading and Phonics..ages 3 to 10

Mathematics..ages 4 to 12

Language..ages 0 to 12

Science, Social Studies, Humanities ....ages 10 and beyond

∙ ∙

Peak daily learning time for
most students ....8:00 am to 10:00 am

Average attention span time
(differs widely) ....Age 7 = 7 minutes
(After 7 years of age, one minute more for each year)

Figure 3-2: Prime Time Learning Periods

Do Prime Times Differ for Gender?

Gender concerns have also been a subject of the research regarding prime times. In the 1960s, the emphasis of the gender issue was equality. The result was that reform occurred in many fields regarding gender discrimination in the form of rule changes and legislation. Now as we observe differences in genetic tendencies we must be careful to avoid stereotyped responses to new information. Because this is a sensitive issue for many, it is best to remain open-minded and continue to be influenced by the statements that all humans have their own unique preferences. Here are some suggested differences noted in recent genetic gender studies (Kimura, 2002).

Suggested Gender-Influenced Prime Times

Male	Female
Better at age 5 in spatial rotation skills	Stronger in verbal memory at age 5
Throwing accuracy develops at age 4	Finger dexterity at age 3
Left hemisphere slow to develop	Left hemisphere develops quickly
Fewer fat cells directly below the skin	Thicker layer of fat directly below skin

Figure 3-3: Gender Differences in Prime Time

We recognize that this research suggests if students are offered appropriate stimuli during these prime times of learning, the information would be stored in the brain and long-term recall would be significant. The way in which we offer that stimulus is important. Research indicates that to increase and improve retention for new material introduced, the lesson must make sense to the learner and in some way be linked to already known material. When this connection happens (meaningful information linked to former memories), we can imagine that the probability of long-term storage is increased. An educator responsible for teaching new information must continually make sure that the steps of connection, the reality of how this information can be useful, and the meaningfulness of the experience are all involved in curriculum and instructional planning. We will further analyze how this process takes place and how to employ long-term memory strategies in Chapter 5.

The teacher who understands more about the individual student he or she is teaching will make a far stronger impact on the student than one who "teaches to the curriculum" or "teaches to the test." If you really want to teach for long-term meaning and recall, then begin to understand your student and provide appropriate experiences that are tailored to the student's learning style and preferential prime times.

Helping Elementary Students Get to Know Their Brains

From the first day of school, let your elementary students know that the activities you plan for them are based on theories about how they learn and develop. Introduce the words **brain-based** and get their feedback on what they think that means. Then do the following activity with your students to get them thinking about their brains:

1. On the first day of school, give each student an enlarged map of the floor plan of your school.

2. Have each student draw on the map where he or she entered the school and draw a line right to the classroom. Then have each student draw his or her desk on the plan.

3. Ask each student to mark a map of his or her own room at home.

4. Discuss with the class that what they are doing is using visual and memory skills to map a learning experience.

5. Now you will show your students how each of their brains maps an experience.

6. Put an outline of the brain on the overhead (from page 38) and use a colored marker to illustrate how a message and thought travels through the brain.

7. Next show students how they can make a model of the brain with their hands.

8. Say, "Place your hands together in a linked grasp with your knuckles touching and your fingers hanging below. Lock your thumbs." Explain that this clasp is close to the actual size of their own brains. Explain that the way their thumbs lock illustrates how the left and right hemispheres intertwine.

Introduce a few key vocabulary words about the brain and relate them to what students already know. Use the short cuts from Figure 3-4 to introduce brain vocabulary to your students. Show them where each center of the brain is located as you introduce it. Relate the more technical terms to real life words for them.

Brain Short Cuts

Brain stem.. heartbeat, sweat, temperature

Cerebellum/Basal ganglia ....jump, dance, walk, move

Limbic system ....feelings, happy, sad, angry, control

Cerebral cortex ....problem solving, compare/contrast

Figure 3-4: Brain Short Cuts

At another time, show your students a video or CD presentation on the brain. There are some excellent CDs and videos to help children understand what is actually occurring in the brain. See the Resources section for more information.

Here's another activity to help your students explore the brain and its workings:

1. Give each student the bottom half of a plastic gallon milk container. (Have an adult cut the container.)

2. Have students paint the container with a grayish-pink paint. Encourage them to use a black marker or paint to draw folds and fissures on the container to duplicate what the brain looks like.

3. Next, work on what is going on inside the brain. Have students write activities they know the brain performs on small strips of paper. Here are some examples to get them started:

   ✔ thinking about math
   ✔ listening
   ✔ paying attention
   ✔ emotions
   ✔ thinking about food
   ✔ dreaming

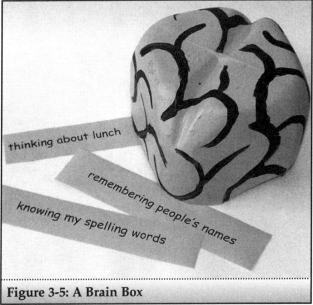

Figure 3-5: A Brain Box

4. Put the slips of paper inside the "brain." Cover the bottom with plastic wrap and secure it with a rubber band. Cut a small slit in the wrap. Now the slips can be removed when needed or more slips can be added.

5. Have students meet in pairs with their brains and discuss what their brains are up to!

Following this brief introduction to the brain, you are ready to get to know each student's individual learning style and personal learning preference. From the basic brain box, we will move, in the next chapter, to understanding student's sensory issues and other factors about their learning, including the choice of their dominant hand and eye.

Use this outline of the brain for the classroom activity on page 36.

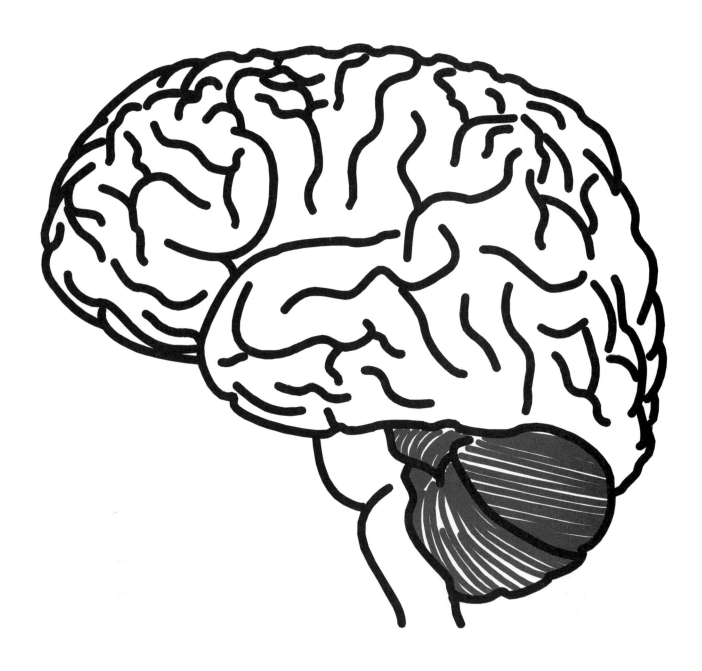

Make the most of yourself,
for that is all there is of you.

—*Ralph Waldo Emerson*

4 The World of the Senses

Sensory Input

Many researchers have attempted to show us the importance of our five senses in helping us learn. Barbe, Swanson, and Sousa are just some of the researchers who have stressed the fact that we each have a preferred learning style. Of the five senses — touch, taste, hearing, seeing, and smell — three primary ones seem to influence learning patterns. The most preferred modalities in teaching academics are visual, auditory, and kinesthetic/tactile. These modalities are often referred to as **VAKT**. If you are using the VAKT guidelines to enhance your students' skills, your instructional style is often described as **multisensory teaching**. This is the type of teaching that incorporates all modalities in the learning environment.

Several publishers offer visual/auditory/tactile tests and surveys you can give your students at any age to determine their own preferences. You can also develop your own survey based on the age range of your students. You will find resources for names of commercial modality questionnaires in the Resources section. You will find one teacher-designed modality preference chart on the next page that you might use as a model for developing your own tool. This survey is a great ice-breaker and "get to know you" activity for the first day of school. First fill out the survey yourself and attach a copy of it to the survey you give each student. Make your own personal sheet a different color so it stands out and children can see that it is yours.

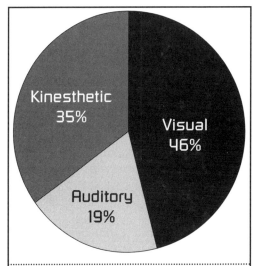

Figure 4-1: The sensory preferences of U.S. student population in grades 3-12 for the mid-1990s (Swanson, 1995; Sousa, 1997, 2001). Reprinted by permission.

Getting to Know You

Name:	Birthday:
Place of birth:	Kind(s) of pet(s):
Name(s) of brother(s):	Name(s) of pet(s):
Name(s) of sister(s):	Hair color:
Circle one: Right-handed Left-handed	Eye color:

What do you think is special about you?

What is one thing about you I wouldn't know just by looking at you?

Tell me your favorite thing in each category.

Food:	Color:
After-school activity:	Music:
Book:	Game:

Put a check (✔) by each thing that describes you.

V	A	KT
❏ I like to use colored pens when I write.	❏ I like to be read to.	❏ I like to draw.
❏ I like to doodle or draw cartoons.	❏ I like to listen to music through headphones.	❏ I can listen and write at the same time.
❏ My room at home is very neat.	❏ I like to tell stories and jokes.	❏ I like to dance.
❏ I like to read.	❏ I like to sing.	❏ I like to draw and make crafts.
❏ I like to write.	❏ I play an instrument.	❏ I like to trace or copy things.

Put a check by the one thing in each row that best describes you.

❏ I express my emotions by the look on my face.	❏ I express my emotion with the sound or volume of my voice.	❏ I express my emotions by the way I sit or stand (posture).
❏ My favorite activities include watching TV or videos or going to a movie.	❏ My favorite activities include listening to music, talking on the phone, or playing an instrument.	❏ My favorite activities include playing outside, riding my bicycle, skateboarding, or anything physical.
❏ If I were an animal, I'd want to be a peacock.	❏ If I were an animal, I'd want to be a parrot.	❏ If I were an animal, I'd want to be a chimpanzee.
❏ I like playing Checkers.	❏ I like playing Charades.	❏ I like playing Twister.
❏ If I were learning something new, I'd rather see it.	❏ If I were learning something new, I'd rather hear about it.	❏ If I were learning something new, I'd rather do it.
❏ It's easy for me to memorize hard words if I see them.	❏ It's easy for me to memorize hard words if I hear or say them.	❏ It's easy for me to memorize hard words if I write them.

Totals		

Total the number of boxes each student checked in each column. The modality with the most number of checks will give you an idea of each student's learning preference. Next tally the students' identifying hand preferences. Present the results to the class in the way of a survey. You might display the results on the chalkboard for everyone to see and say the following:

> "70% of our class members are right-handers. 30% are left-handers. If you are a left-hander you may sit in the marked desks, as they will be more helpful to you in your writing. Also, left-handed scissors are available in our art corner."

You might address the learning style portion of the survey by saying something like this:

> "The majority of our classmates prefer visual materials when they learn something new. I will be using an overhead, or visuals on the board in every lesson. If you enjoy drawing, I will ask you to help me out with these visuals on the board, on paper, and by decorating our room."

You can employ the data you have gathered in multiple ways. You may wish to use it to set up small social groups and study groups. Placing students with similar characteristics on a team (all visual learners, for example) can help inspire team spirit and dedication. The team members immediately feel they have something in common with one another.

Here are some other ways to address learning styles and intelligence types in the classroom:

1. Give each child a colored dot to identify the way he or she learns. (Identify one color for each modality and keep the color consistent in all materials and uses. For example, use pink for visual, blue for auditory, and green for kinesthetic/tactile. Divide students into groups by modality.

2. Ask for your students' VAKT input into an activity. You might say something like, "I have just put a vocabulary word and definition on the board. Visual learners? How can I help you understand this word better? What could I add to the board for you?

3. On instructing the class in a science lesson you might state, "This activity (example: classifying plant types) will require all my naturalists in the class to act as our coaches. If there is any way you see that you can add something to this lesson with your expertise, please raise your hand."

4. Upon teaching the spelling of the word "Mississippi," you might appeal to the auditory learners by saying, "Musical/rhythmic people, help us develop a beat or pattern to easily learn the spelling of this word."

5. You can involve spatial learners in changing the room arrangement by saying, "Spatial learners I need you to stay with me after class for just a few minutes to help me design an area where we can put our new computer in the room."

One exceptional second grade teacher I know starts the first day of the school year by giving each child a sheet of paper on which is written the following:

Hair color: _____   Eye color: _____

What is special about you? _____

There is room left on the sheet for a face drawing. She then has each child complete the information and the picture and places it in a large basket. Gathering the class around her, she draws one paper at a time and tries to guess which child made the page. When she guesses a child correctly, she writes the student's name on the paper in that person's favorite color and places it on a bulletin board labeled "Found: New Friends!"

This identifying of specific learning styles and adapting the environment for them will become contagious! Children will feel more open about discussing their individual learning preferences and your modeling will help them use their strengths to help others.

You can assess a student's preferred method of learning on the computer also. A software package, *Learning Styles Inventory* (2001), provides you with a program that can individually determine each student's learning style preference. Your student completes a questionnaire on the screen and the results are tabulated. You can also get a profile of the entire class, which will allow you to set up group or teamwork situations based on modalities. As an added bonus there is a teacher profile that helps you determine your own style. See the Resource section for more information.

Eye Movement and Processing Information

Bandler and Grinder (1979) were one of the first groups of researchers to begin looking at nonverbal cues and cognitive processing. This research is described as **neurolinguistic programming**. The techniques of this research used eye movement as a tool for understanding how it helps us determine individual VAKT preferences.

In her book, *A Framework for Understanding Poverty*, Ruby Payne describes the main concepts of this technique. Payne notes, "Think of the human face as a clock. To begin, the face has three zones. When a person's gaze is directed in the top

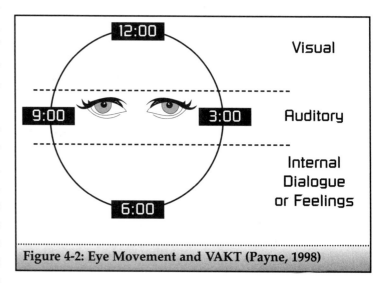

Figure 4-2: Eye Movement and VAKT (Payne, 1998)

zone, the individual is processing VISUAL information. When eyes are in the middle zone, the individual is processing AUDITORY information (with one exception). When eyes are in the bottom zone, the individual is either talking to himself/herself or processing feelings" (Payne, 1998).

Visual Processing

If a right-handed person is looking at the 2:00, then that individual is processing visually remembered data. Around 10:00, the individual is processing visually constructed data. In other words, the individual is putting together data from several sources. If the person is left-handed, then 2:00 represents visually constructed data, and 10:00 is visually remembered data.

Auditory Processing

If the person is right-handed, the 3:00 position indicates remembered auditory information and the 9:00 position indicates constructed auditory information. If the individual is left-handed, then 3:00 is auditory constructed and 9:00 is auditory remembered.

Kinesthetic Processing

If the individual is right-handed, the 5:00 position is auditory internal dialogue, and the 7:00 position is feelings. If the individual is left-handed, then 5:00 is feelings, while 7:00 is auditory dialogue.

If the eyes are staring straight ahead and defocused, the individual is in a visual construct pattern.

Eye movement can help a teacher with VAKT information. If a student has moved his or her eyes to a visual position, then the teacher is alerted that the student is trying to find a visual cue to process the information. The teacher can then encourage the learning process by asking the student, "What do you see? What image can you envision." If the student is observed to be in the middle zone, thus processing from an auditory position, the teacher can offer, "What do you remember hearing?" Finally, if the student lowers their eyes and avoids any contact, the teacher is made aware that the student may be processing or working on feelings. Eye movements can help the teacher identify how a student tends to store and retrieve information (Payne, 1998, pp. 120-131).

Left-handed vs. Right-handed Students

In our classroom population today, right-handers make up about 90% of the school-age population. Of all the primates, only humans display such a strong predisposition to right-handedness (Hotz, 2002a). Handedness is established in the fetus by the fifteenth week of gestation.

You have probably seen stores or catalogs selling materials specifically for people who are left-handed. As a classroom teacher, language therapist, or related service professional you have no doubt provided left-handed scissors for your students with that preference, and perhaps suggested that their seat placement be on the outside of the row so they can copy more easily without bumping arms with a right-handed classmate.

Recent research at UCLA, specifically looking at left- and right-handers, has suggested that there is a noticeable difference in the brains of people who are left-handed. Their brains are more symmetrical than right-handers. In fact, the two sides are more equal in a left-handed person. This finding indicates there is more flexibility in the brain structure of people who grow up left-handed. Researchers found that the hereditary difference between right-handers and left-handers appears to affect how the brain changes in size throughout a lifetime. They found indications that right-handers typically have a larger left-brain hemisphere, which is where their language abilities are concentrated. Conversely, left-handers have more balanced brains, with both sides relatively symmetrical. The language abilities of left-handers more often are concentrated on the right side of the brain (Hotz, 2002c).

> "Recent research . . . has suggested that there is a noticeable difference in the brains of people who are left-handed."

There is information that notes a student's pattern of hand/foot/eye dominance. The majority of people tend to have one-sided dominance. One-sided dominance is described as the use of all one-sided preferences of hand, eye, and foot. It occurs when an individual shows a clear-cut inclination for a hand, foot, or eye. The selection of all one-sided dominance seems to indicate the strongest and most fluid learning style.

When dominance preference is described as "crossed," the dominant hand and the dominant eye are on opposite sides. An individual demonstrates "crossed" dominance when there is no preference or advantage of one side over the other. For example, they may be right-handed but left-eyed. Individuals with reading difficulties may exhibit crossed dominance. Crossed dominance concerning handedness and eyedness is considered to be detrimental in developing a smooth and fluid reading style.

You can easily test which dominant eye and hand your students prefer. Follow these steps to determine eye preference:

1. Collect a box of 20 different objects that require one eye or monocular vision (paper towel tube, telescope, 3" x 5" card with a small hole in it, a large needle with an eye, etc.).

2. Have each student look with one eye through the openings of the objects.

3. Record which eye the student uses for each task. The eye most frequently selected is the dominant eye.

Follow a similar procedure to test for hand preference. Have each student manipulate 20 different objects or perform tasks that require one-handed skill (using a pencil or a fork, turning a doorknob, waving, shaking hands, etc.). The hand most frequently used is the dominant hand.

Organizational and Record-Keeping Tips

You can implement some basic organization cues to help yourself be more aware of individual learning preferences. These approaches will help you to easily incorporate brain-based teaching techniques into the learning environment.

Coding the Class List

Color-code individual learning characteristics alongside students' names in your plan book. List their modality preferences in learning and their handedness. Choose one color for each grouping. For example, identify visual learners by highlighting their names in pink, auditory learners in blue, and kinesthetic/tactile learners in green. Select an additional color, such as purple, for students who do not display a specific dominant learning preference but seem to use them all.

To further support your ability to respond to your students' needs, note other critical pieces of information with abbreviations. For example, code all students who have an Individual Educational Plan with the initials "IEP" and students for whom a Section 504 (students who requires specific accommodations based on their needs) is in place, with "504." Title I math could be represented as "T1M." Do the same for any students receiving related services such as occupational therapy (OT) or speech language therapy (ST). You should also specifically code each child according to hand preference. You might use "R" for right-handers and "L" for left-handers. Now you will be able to simply scan your grade book and know individual needs by color and code.

Samantha Aaron   R
(highlighted in pink for visual learning style)

Taylor Adams   R IEP ST
(highlighted in green for kinesthetic/tactile learning style)

Justin Austin   R
(highlighted in blue for auditory learning style)

Raul Blanca   R
(highlighted in purple for no learning style preference)

Jake Bloomberg   L 504 T1M
(highlighted in pink for visual learning style)

Figure 4-3: Example of class list using highlighting for modality, letter for handedness, and code for services.

Organize Your Daily Planner

Take your own daily lesson plan book and color code wide bands to identify the ways you are addressing each modality. Repeat the color examples you used for the names in your class list (pink for visual, blue for auditory, green for kinesthetic, purple for all modalities). This color-coding strategy provides a cue for your brain to remember to include activities that support each modality in your plans. It will add a successful and quick way for you to identify how you are including these learning styles. Here is an example of a daily planner that is organized by learning style. Note: Imagine each row is highlighted in a color to reflect that particular modality.

Day	Monday	Tuesday	Wednesday	Thursday	Friday
Subject	50 minutes language arts: Introduce *Charlotte's Web*.	Review yesterday's introduction: have students share what they liked best about the book so far. Read the next chapter.	Have three students review their impression of the chapters read.	Post web of book's characters on overhead and review what has occurred so far.	Invite former student, librarian, or guest to review with students the first chapters of the book with them and note their own favorite parts.
Visual	Use word web on the chalkboard to introduce the characters.	Display the web of characters on an overhead. Have students vote on which character they think is most interesting, most unlikely to be their friend, etc. Color code their responses by vote (Most popular color blue, etc.).	Have each student make a bookmark that includes the title, author, characters, conflict, resolution, and summary. Have them place the mark in their books and add information as it occurs.	Have students find a comfortable place in the room, hall, or school library where they can independently read the next chapter.	Display pictures of characters from the book on slides or Power Point. At the same time, have the next chapter on tape for students to listen to.
Auditory	Play a tape of characters acting out the first chapter.	Set up a listening corner with the book on tape available.	Have students read aloud the next chapter using both choral reading and individual readers.	Place the name of a character on each student's desk. When they return from reading, they must get in the group with other students who have the same character name. Discuss that character within the group.	Have students interview guest and ask questions about the book.
Kinesthetic	Have students make a picture of what they think the barnyard portrayed in Chapter 1 looks like.	Mount pictures for students to observe. Have students label what they drew with the corresponding page in the book where the scene occurred.	Allow students to doodle and draw on a plain white sheet marked "idea sheet" as they listen to someone reading orally. Suggest doodles be about what they are listening to.	In their character groups, students must come up with three statements about their character and what they would change about them.	Have students make a mosaic (small, colored pieces of torn paper) of a spider web.

Figure 4-4: Example of lesson plan addressing different learning styles

Identifying Students' Needs

Another helpful way to identify students quickly is to put each child's name on a color-coded 3" x 5" index card. For example, Taylor, the student noted in Figure 4-3, would be on a green card to reflect her preference for kinesthetic learning. Keep the cards in a box on your desk. When you are calling on students for input, select a colored card to help you tailor the question to the student's learning needs. To be even more selective, separate the cards into groups according to learning style. When you need an answer that is primarily based on visual information you can call on a student for whom visual information is a strength. If the question involves auditory expertise, then you select a student who has demonstrated a preference for auditory learning. Your selection will be random (by color only, not name), thus allowing you to call on students in a fair manner and avoid calling on the same students frequently.

Maintaining Students' Papers

To further complement your planner and grade book, create simple paper folders in the four learning style identification colors in which to keep students' papers. Make a folder for each student that corresponds to his or her respective modality color by folding a sheet of 11" x 17" colored construction paper in half. Put finished and graded papers in the folders and share them at conference time with parents. The color-coding offers a way to begin to educate parents on what you have learned about their child's individual learning style preference.

A Gift for Your Brain

You will be delighted by how quickly your own brain will absorb and pick up on these techniques for identifying students. Very rapidly you will be thinking in a color-coded mode. These initial and simple strategies provide an organizational framework for your entire year and create an atmosphere for teaching the "whole child." Not only will you benefit from a system of color coding, but so will your students. Provide them with colored laminated plastic paper (that correspond to their individual learning preferences), and have them place the papers on or in classroom texts. This allows students to color code their books for easy recall and order. You will be surprised how easy it is for students to find books and materials when they use color-coded techniques.

Understanding Student Preferences

Now that you have identified your students' preferred learning styles and characteristics, and have set up a simple way to recognize these choices in your class, here is information to help you learn more about each predilection. These specifics will help you move forward to learning more about each modality.

I see you!

Visual learners tend to respond best when a teacher offers visual stimuli to accompany the auditory presentation. They benefit from information through words with pictures, and they are quickly forming their own visuals in their mind as you speak. Call on them to enhance what you are saying with their visual interpretation.

Visual learners benefit in the classroom from the following:

- graphs and charts
- webs and mapping
- overhead projectors
- lists on the chalkboard
- computer screens
- handouts
- maps and posters
- cue cards
- outlines
- number lines

When you can add illustrations as you speak, you double the possibilities of recall for these students. They may listen to you while doodling or taking notes. You will spot them visually "looking up" at your alphabet strips, cue cards, and maps as they work to seek visual support. Important factor: Visual learners benefit more from *actually making* the visuals themselves to accompany the work, rather than you providing premade ones them for them. Here are some other characteristics of visual learners:

- They keep their eyes on you often and turn to you when you move in the room.
- At times you see them close their eyes or look away as they try to recall visual pictures.
- They notice what people wear and make comments about others' expressions and facial gestures.
- They model and mimic gestures and prefer your visual gestures, hand movements, and visual expressions to other kinds of information.

- They are quick to "judge the book by its cover" because they rely so much on visual input.
- They may read better silently than orally.

I listen!

Auditory learners learn by talking to themselves, talking with others, and by listening. Here are some characteristics of auditory learners:

- They may move their lips as they try to memorize or read.
- They want to discuss, review, and discuss again.
- They can often accurately repeat musical patterns, dialects, accents, etc.
- They will find success in group discussions, oral reports, and verbal discourse throughout the day.
- They will benefit from directions that offer a summary and verbal analysis rather than details.
- They often are spotted talking to themselves or humming.
- They appreciate activities that incorporate role-playing, acting out, and group-based activities like vote-taking.
- They often lose their place when reading and may have trouble with sight vocabulary.

I need touch!

Kinesthetic or tactile learners need to have it, touch it, do it! Here are some characteristics of kinesthetic learners:

- They want to own, use, and manipulate objects.
- Give them a box of cubes and they will finger each cube and probably rearrange them in the box.
- Hand them a pencil and they will tap it on the table as they listen.
- They may write in the air or on their hand with their finger.
- They engage others with their touch and move often in their seats as they work.
- They require more breaks and will pay more attention to what's going *on* in a story rather than to details about the characters.
- They will ask, "What are we going to do next?" if the pace seems slow or tiresome.
- Some have developed their own "out of sight" ways to handle their need for movement — tapping their foot, twisting their hair, etc.

- They are often up on their knees, turning their chairs around as they sit, and are the first ones out the door at recess.

- They may not remember things well even when continued rehearsal is used

- They use gestures when they speak.

- They often display characteristics of both the auditory and visual learner.

Are some students a combination or blend of all modalities? Of course! What we know is we are more apt to rely on a variety of modalities at any one time but *favor* one when we are in the actual process of learning.

A recent imaging study compared reading and listening activities in the brain. Michael and colleagues (2001) found that the brain processes information differently depending on how the information is communicated. They found that when subjects listened to a sentence (received auditory information), a different pathway was activated than when subjects read the same words printed on paper. They found that the total amount of activation was greater in the auditory activity than in the visual activity. Auditory stimulus seemed to present greater activation in both right and left hemispheres. This demonstrated that there is more semantic processing and working memory recall in listening comprehension than in sight-reading alone.

The following pages contain some specific information about meeting the needs of different learning types in your classroom.

The Visual Learner

What the visual learner requires:	What the teacher offers:
Clear visual cues	drawings, charts, worksheets
To see the big picture	webbing, mapping, graphic organizers
To see the action	a seat near activity
Information on overhead, board	number and visual cues on chalkboard or overhead for easy copying
Opportunity to jot or write	color code, use *Frameworks*®
Praise	stickers, notes home, point charts

Frameworks are commercially made webs and maps that can be used by students for note-taking. The web or map allows the student to "visualize" the main idea and develop the written format from this structure. See information on *Frameworks* in the Resources section.

When they do not understand your instruction:
Visual learners will look puzzled, squint, and appear to be daydreaming.

Additional tools to help the visual learner:
- Student should type words on the computer and print them out.
- Teach students to doodle or add visual images to information they are trying to learn.
- Students will often appear to daydream when directions are given. Involve the students with participation-type activities to engage their attention.
- Use colored flash cards for rehearsal or vocabulary words and have the student illustrate the card for recall. (Example: Nouns are blue, proper nouns are green.)
- Use calculators with large displays and graph paper for math problems.
- Use pictures for story starters.

The Auditory Learner

What the auditory learner requires:	What the teacher offers:
Clear auditory directions	brief, to-the-point verbal cues, overhead
Oral expression opportunities	oral book reports, discussion groups
Listening to oral presentations	tape recorder, tapes, videos, recorded reading assignments
Auditory mnemonics	break words into syllable patterns, offer verbal cues to tasks (I before E, except after C)
Praise	verbal compliments specific to the task
Help with sight word vocabulary	phonics programs with emphasis on making sounds and taping them

When they do not understand your instruction:
Auditory learners will begin to talk to themselves.

Additional tools to help the auditory learner:
- Calculators with voice capability
- Computer programs that incorporate sound
- Computer text-to-speech or Kurzweil® readers
- Reading aloud whenever possible
- Cover sheet or file folder with a "reading window" cut into it to eliminate too much visual stimulation on page
- Instructing student to sub-vocalize (say it aloud in his or her head)

The Kinesthetic Learner

What the kinesthetic learner requires:	*What the teacher offers:*
Hands-on activities	movement, breaks, textbook, workbook
Opportunity to manipulate	Items that provide tactile stimulation, such as Wikki-Stix®, Koosh® balls, sandpaper squares
Quick writing activities	computer programs such as Alpha Smart®
Physical movement	role-playing, seat changes, experiments
Praise	touch, pat on the back, fill-in wall chart
Help remembering things	multiple memory tricks, less reliance on rote

When they do not understand your instruction:

Kinesthetic learners start fidgeting, moving around, and looking for something to touch.

Additional tools to help the kinesthetic learner:

- Multiple techniques that were listed for both auditory and visual learner
- Mechanical devices such as Palm® Pilots, computers, hand-held calculators, gadgets
- Role-playing and acting out experiences and stories they have read.
- Instructing student to sub-vocalize (say it aloud in his or her head)

Take me to your memory!

Memory Strategies

You've probably had a memory experience similar to this one: you are standing at the kitchen sink and say to yourself, "I need to go to the mall, but I do not have any cash, so I better get my checkbook in the bedroom before I leave." You then head to the bedroom and find yourself asking, "Why am I here?" You can't remember why you went to your bedroom! So what do you do next? You probably try to visualize where you were last and what you had been doing. You might return to the sink and go through the same steps again hoping to trigger the memory. When the memory of "checkbook" reoccurred, you may even have walked back to the bedroom saying aloud, "Checkbook, checkbook, checkbook!" You used all your senses and strategies to bring back the missing thought. The activation of memory is not just a single process but rather a series of different interactive processes in our brain.

For centuries, researchers and philosophers have examined and debated the phenomenon of memory. They have encouraged the study of how the brain accomplishes this very rudimentary of mental functions. We all may have different levels of ability, varied interests, and different needs but we all work, handle information, and exist within the function of our memory.

How Is a Memory Created?

The memory process is a series of interactive steps that occur the minute we are exposed to new information. Like an electrical series, the brain grasps the new information and sends it on a pre-wired pathway. The brain has a specific pattern encoded to where the incoming message will go. When the brain receives the new information — if you have the right connection and it is presented at the right time — the information will be stored for future use.

The most important task in memory involvement is your brain's ability to retrieve the memory and use it in any situation. The storage or retrieval of memory is considered the function of your long-term memory. Long-term memory includes recalling a combination of events in your life.

Nobel Prize winner Eric Kandel's research on memory has identified two separate areas of the brain where storage for long-term memory exists. He feels each area of the brain collects a specific type of recall. Dr. Kandel identifies the two areas as the following:

- **explicit memory storage**
  This is where the brain stores conscious recall of information about people, objects and places, and the things we see every day

- **implicit memory storage**
  This includes the unconscious recall of perceptual and motor skills. Implicit memory storage is further described as the capacity for learning skills and procedures, including those used in playing a sport or dancing.

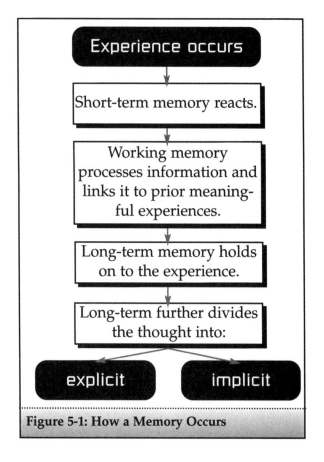

Figure 5-1: How a Memory Occurs

Other researchers have described these two overlapping systems by labeling explicit as **declarative** memory and implicit as **nondeclarative** memory (Patoine, 2001).

Declarative, or explicit, memory is the ability to store and recall information that we can describe verbally or write about. This would include facts, data, names, faces, places we have been, and things we see every day. Nondeclarative, or implicit, memory is the procedural or hands-on recall that helps us actually "do" what we have learned. Memory studies have shown that about a third of healthy older people have difficulty with nondeclarative memory, yet a substantial number of

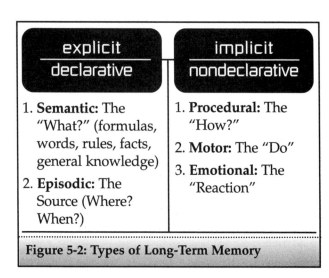

Figure 5-2: Types of Long-Term Memory

80-year olds perform *as well as* people in their 30s on declarative memory tests (Patoine, 2001).

The ability to store and retrieve memories is greatest during the prime times of zero through 18 years of age, then around age 40 there is a slight decline in memory. The most dramatic decline in memory is *after* age seventy.

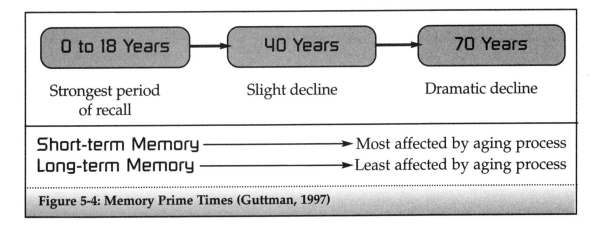

Figure 5-4: Memory Prime Times (Guttman, 1997)

Memory In the Classroom

It is critical that as an educator you help students remember and be able to produce what they have learned. Therefore, it should be your goal to instill the type of learning that allows students to encode information into long-term memory. This type of processing will occur if you can help students create solid memories of the information.

Here are some ways to help you get students to move the information you teach into their long-term memories:

- *Connect:* When you introduce new material, provide a link to what students already know.

- *Make it real:* Break the new information down into the most basic, sensible presentation.

- *Make it meaningful:* Show how the information connects to what students already know and what they want to know.

Real-World Learning
A student teacher I was supervising had introduced 15 vocabulary words to a group of 22 fifth graders. She passed out the list of new words and asked students to look up the definition of each word and use the word in a descriptive sentence. When the papers were completed and handed in, the student teacher was dismayed and disappointed to find that the sentences were not

more interesting! For example, for the word *desire* several students had sub-mitted the sentence "I desire it." She told me she thought the students did not really read the dictionary definitions, for she felt had they done so they would have written more creative sentences. She felt they needed more vocabulary drills to allow their language to expand and to be more inventive. I gently explained to her that my impression was that when they looked up the words in the dictionary, they were unable to find a link to what they already knew. The result was a sentence written *around* a definition. I advised that she go back and introduce each word in a sentence that would be meaningful for this age group and made the following suggestions to guide her sentence creation:

- Use sentences that are age relevant and offer timely links to the students' environment and interests.

- Include class members' names in the examples and associate the sentences to those students' interests and personalities.

- Have the students write their own sentences following her introduction of the meaningful sentences and use the dictionary at the end of the lesson to check appropriateness of word usage.

As a result of following the above suggestions, the students' next attempt at sentence writing produced examples that were vastly diverse and included a variety of expansion words, adjectives, and creative expressions. The students appeared to know the words and were later observed using them in their own conversations.

Impact of Seat Placement on Memory and Testing

An educator or therapist is immediately building memories for the student the minute he or she starts teaching a class. Where we stand, what we wear, and how we teach are all part of the memory process. The child will use all these learning observations to help remember what is being taught. For example, I once tutored a high school student who was having difficulty remembering a certain formula that had been introduced in his chemistry class. I began to review the formula and reminded him that his teacher had told me he introduced this formula two days ago. The student then exclaimed, "Oh, now I remember — that was the day he had mustard all over his shirt! Now I know what you are talking about!" From that day on we referred to that formula as the MUSTARD. Do not lose sight of the fact that memory is created by experience; therefore, even where a child sits in the room during a lesson impacts the learning experience.

> ". . . changing a student's seat placement in class the day of a test results in poorer test performance."

Research studies have demonstrated that changing a student's seat placement in class the day of a test results in poorer test performance. If the student remains in the same seat where they were when he or she learned the information, a higher score results. Why is this? Because, as we have discovered, learning is a process and many experiences make up the learning activity. The student sat in that seat and watched you introduce the lesson, observed your manner and your clothes, listened to the sounds and words you used, and saw and watched others' reactions — all the while learning new information. It was a *total* learning experience. *All* of that sensory input added to the student's memories for the topic you were teaching. Therefore, it is critical to present as many of the same experiences as possible when testing the information as you did when you were teaching it. If a student tries to recall the information he learned during the testing process, his working mind will remember the information more readily if there are immediate associations from the initial teaching environment present.

Ways to Strengthen Memory Encoding

There has been some research indicating that if an activity occurs during the learning process that incorporates intensive emotions, such as drama or joy, into the activity, the brain may release adrenaline that allows memory to be encoded in an even stronger format. Cowley and Underwood (1998) call this memory process **elaborative encoding**. They suggest that the brain takes information and links it to what we already know. They note our brains are not designed to retain random bits of information; rather, our brain links or encodes new information to what we already know or have emotionally experienced.

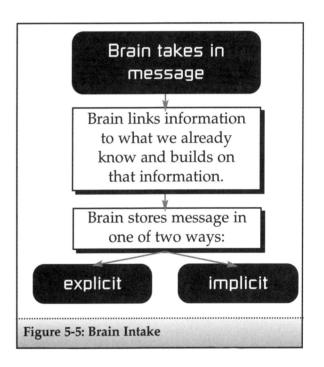

Figure 5-5: Brain Intake

Have you ever observed the "aha!" effect in your classroom when, during instruction, you see the light bulb go on in a student's eyes? You know they understand the concept of what you are teaching. My impression is that what you are seeing is the actual encoding of the idea as it "fires up" in the brain.

According to Levine (1994), here are some ways to encourage the use of elaborative encoding in the activities we teach.

1. Mental pictures
2. Linguistic information
3. Physical sensations
4. Emotions

- **Mental pictures**

  Most people form their own mental images as they are listening to information. Try this experiment: say the words *Bali Hai* in front of a group of adults and ask them what images those words conjure. You will be amazed at the diversity of answers. In my experiment with these words I have heard some of the following: an island, a type of bra, a local restaurant, and a woman singing on a beach. Everyone in my group had his or her own separate encoding for the word. Now relate this experience to when you are teaching a class. You introduce a vocabulary word and *assume* that everyone understands the way you comprehend the word. However, if we understand elaborative encoding, we recognize that everyone puts his or her own experience with the word to work. To teach a concept or new vocabulary word, make sure everyone achieves the same mental picture. Provide the visual you want to convey along with the word. This extra step will result in the same encoding experience for the entire class. You have heard the expression "We're on the same page." The theory of mental pictures is that we all recognize the same mental image to help us remember.

  Teacher's Memory Tip: To remember specific information tied to the curriculum we must all start with the same mental image of what we are to learn.

- **Linguistic information**

  Another way to add elaborative encoding is to add linguistic information to the memory task. Many people rely on the linguistic pattern or sound of what they are trying to recall in order to remember information. For example, there is an entire generation of students who have watched the TV show *Seinfeld*, and when you say "yadda, yadda, yadda" (a popular phrase used on the show) they will associate immediate meaning to the words. They encoded a linguistic memory. The auditory part of the message brought back recall of the meaning for them. Therefore, when we teach, we want to create linguistic memories by using figurative language, changing the intonation and inflection of our voices, and using key phrases that link immediate and long-term memories.

  Teacher's Memory Tip: Use phrases, patterns of words, and interesting word combinations to increase recall for linguistic memory.

- **Physical sensations**
  Actual physical sensations add to the memory experience. It's important to know that aroma, smells, and touch or movement can assist in creating learning memories. Most students can remember what it "felt" like when a teacher accidentally scraped a nail or sharp instrument on a chalkboard. The physical sensation of that sound can evoke for some the exact impression and "feel " of the experience! Smell is especially impressionable on the mind and people will often share how a certain perfume or bakery aroma brings back memories. One way to introduce the physical sensation of smell into your instruction is to allow students to use scented markers to help encode information and recall memories that the fragrances evoke.

  > **Teacher's Memory Tip:** Actual aromas and physical sensations introduced into instruction can help students encode strong memory connections and evoke past memories.

- **Emotions**
  The last of the four ways to add encoding pathways in memory is the experience of emotion. Certain familiarity can have such emotional impact that we can keep in mind the exact emotional/physical response we had many years later. For example, think of a time when you won something or celebrated a very important accomplishment in your life. When something like it occurs again, or someone even describes a similar occurrence, the immediate emotions you had during the initial experience return. The same feeling you sensed when you received the honor comes back and the memory becomes very physical in nature. We can add an arousing climate to our classroom and teaching situation by providing an environment that is both positive and nurturing. We can stimulate a mood and spirit in our classrooms that the student relates to security and success.

  > **Teacher's Memory Tip:** Encourage a positive, proactive feeling when you introduce new material. This will stimulate positive emotional memory making for your students.

Remembering Explicit Information

You can help your students remember explicit information, such as names and addresses, by using multiple encoding strategies. Research has shown that students remember simple facts if a variety of tools are used to introduce those facts.

An article in the American Psychological Association's, July 30, 2001 issue of *Experimental Psychology* featured a research study that looked at a way to help students remember names. The researchers introduced two groups of students to people by name. The first group of students was asked to write each new person's name. The second group was asked to associate each person's name with a mental picture and a linguistic cue.

One year later everyone returned to the research site and and researchers asked the two groups if they could remember the names of the people they met a year ago. Everyone in the second group remembered the names and no one in the first group did! This experiment demonstrated the significance of using multiple encoding strategies in the memory process.

> **Teacher's Memory Tip:** To encourage your students to remember the material you are teaching you must employ ways for the brain to remember it.

Encouraging Memory Recall

Here are six positive ways to stimulate and engage memory recall:

1. *Rehearsal:* repeat it, say it, see it, do it again
2. *Association:* link it, find a similar theme, find what's similar
3. *The loci technique:* make it *local* to what you know
4. *Concept imaging:* visualize a concept and exaggerate it
5. *Color:* color-code materials for subject areas, using color for emphasis
6. *Mnemonics:* tricks, devices and patterns to engage the brain

1. *Rehearsal*

Typically, the average teacher will first suggest rehearsal to students as a tool for memory. You can probably remember your own teachers telling you, "Do it, do it again and you will remember it," or "Write it 100 times and then you will know it." What we have learned is that *the way* you rehearse is what helps us remember, not just the repeated practice. David Sousa (2001a) states, "practice does not make perfect, it makes permanent" (p. 124). He further states that material should be learned in small chunks or in a short format.

For practice to be a successful technique, the teacher needs to add unique information to the memory task. Repeated practice can be boring. That is why the use of variety or novelty enhances learning for rote information. In order for practice to be successful, it needs to be unique. It should incorporate a disciplined, structured manner of repeating the information that is lively and interesting for the student. Repeating it the same way over and over can create a "tune-out situation" or passive state in the student's brain. See the example on the next page.

You say:	apple, apple, apple, apple
Brain response:	*Huh? What were you saying? I don't remember.*
Instead, you say:	APP—le, ap—ple, A—PP—le! APPLE

Now the brain is interested and begins to encode the process.

Further ideas for rehearsal:

✔ *Use a plan to practice spelling or vocabulary words.* Present a different activity for each day you are studying the words and incorporate all learning modalities. Here's an example of a student practice plan:

1. *Day one:* Read the word in a meaningful sentence.

2. *Day two:* Break the word into chunks using a set of manipulative or magnetic letters. Try to spell out each word in these letters.

3. *Day three:* Spell the words aloud into a tape recorder using an animated, interesting voice for each word. Play the tape back as you look at the words.

4. *Day four:* Write the words using different media — colored pen on dry erase board, ink pen on brown or colored paper, etc.

5. *Day five:* Cover letters randomly to see if you can quickly recall which ones are missing.

6. *Day six:* Ace the spelling/vocabulary test!

✔ *Make interactive flash cards for new words.* Many students use flash cards to help review and rehearse a word and its definition. Unfortunately, flash card use only affects one modality and as a result, may only impact short-term memory and not send the word into long-term memory. The person using this technique may know the word for the test but not know it two days later. To use rehearsal to stimulate the brain's ability to take the word into long-term memory, try the following technique:

1. Gather several different colors of 3" x 5" index cards. Decide how you will sort your words by color. For example, you might use blue cards for nouns, green for adverbs, etc. Another technique is to categorize by function. Use pink to represent words associated with people, green for animals, etc.

2. Write the word you are trying to learn on one side of an appropriately-colored card and the definition on the other.

3. Now it is time to chunk the word into small parts and see what your brain already recognizes. Examine the word and see if there is a key word or what looks like a "part" of a word you already recognize. Build on this pre-learned experience to help you create a long-term memory for the word.

4. Try to find a cue in the letters that will link the meaning to the definition. For example, imagine the word is *apex*, which means highest point. Underline *ape*, which reminds you of an ape, and then visualize an ape climbing to the highest point of a building in the same way King Kong scaled the Empire State building. To add further recall, draw a small picture of an ape on a building on the front of the card.

5. In the steps above you have used visualization, illustration and chunking (word parts) to help you remember a word. Use these approaches with the other words you wrote on cards.

✔ *Break word lists into chunks or brief groups of information when you practice.* Teach students to always break lists of words or columns of vocabulary into chunks or smaller groups. The smaller pieces of information are more manageable for the brain to process, and they will be able to remember them more readily. Present stimulation and episodic memory techniques to your students when rote material must be learned. Model for them how to put similar words into groups or categories for easier recall. For example, here is a typical list of vocabulary words that might come from a chapter in an action book:

leader	challenge	survivor
mango	scorpion	confrontation
snake	tree frog	members
initiative	citrus	oysters

Show your students how the list can be divided into threes by grouping words that share some sort of association (spelling, meaning, structure, category, etc.). Here is one way the list above might be broken down and an explanation of why these words were put together:

Word Group	Association
leader, survivor, members	group-related terms
citrus, oysters, mango	food
scorpion, snake, tree frog	animals
confrontation, initiative, challenge	goal-oriented words

Tell your students that this technique creates an identity for the words that allows the brain to encode the information more rapidly and accurately. The words do not appear separate but are linked in a similar way that adds recall. Chunking word lists makes long-term recall of individual words more successful.

The size of the group or chunk is best introduced by using three like items in a group first and then increasing to five, seven, and eventually, ten, as skill and ability increase. The chunking technique can work on any rote memorization item, including words, phrases, and dates. To further enhance recall and add other modality preferences, have students make colored flash cards of the groups of words, read them orally, and try to visualize their relationships.

This technique takes common rehearsal and makes it more novel, thereby, appealing to the specific needs of the brain. In this way, we are using elaborative encoding to link what we already know to what we need to know. Eric Jensen wrote in 1996, "The brain likes novelty. It is intrigued by it and pays attention to it."

Teacher tip to enhance rehearsal: Add meaning, novelty, and depth to the rehearsal of material and you will increase memory.

2. *Association*

Association is the ability to help the mind associate what works and can have meaning. Read the following paragraph to yourself:

> A newspaper is better than a magazine, and a seashore is a better place than a street. At first, it is better to run than to walk. Also, you may have to try it several times. It takes some skill but it is easy to learn. Even young children can enjoy it. Once successful, complications are minimal. Birds seldom get too close. One needs lots of room. Too many people doing the same thing can also cause problems. If there are no complications, it can be very peaceful. A rock will serve as an anchor. If things break loose from it however, you will not get a second chance.
>
> (Bransford & Johnson, 1972, in Lerner, 1988, p. 360)

Now ask yourself, "What is the *main idea* of that paragraph?" If you are struggling to find the meaning of what was just read, you are not alone! You certainly can read all the words but there is no meaning or no link to what it may mean for you. What is missing is an association to what you already know. Let's help the brain out. The title of the above paragraph is *Kites*. Now go back and read the paragraph again. You should be able to make more sense of it this time around. As you read it this time, you will experience your brain visualizing a kite and should actually feel how your brain encodes memories for you.

To help your students experience the "connection of association," try the following:

✔ When introducing new vocabulary words, incorporate them into meaningful sentences. Never introduce a vocabulary word alone or list a word alone without putting it into an engaging sentence. The sentence will add meaning and association to the word, making it memorable to the brain.

✔ Find what the student already knows about the information and build the teaching base from there.

✔ Link memories to meaningful and multisensory experiences. For example, when you are teaching about apples, provide apples, have students eat apples, compare the different flavors of apples, show pictures of apples before and after blooming, pass out apple seeds, etc. Have your students create songs, poems, and stories about apples and give them opportunities to tell one another what they have learned about apples. Record their experiences using audio, visual, and print media. Here are some other activities to introduce that involve multiple modalities:

  • Act out stories about farmers planting and harvesting apples.

  • Make a time line of apple growth.

  • Post a classroom calendar where students can record when apples should be planted and when they might be ready to pick.

This array of activities based on one theme is a prime example of associating every experience to all modalities and providing the brain with associations that will turn into long-term memories.

✔ Before giving students a reading assignment, use meaningful contexts to review new vocabulary words they will encounter in the reading assignment. Students need to understand new vocabulary words and how they relate to their lives before they can read a chapter with success.

> **Teacher tip for using association techniques:** Help students link what they do not know to what they do know for recollection.

3. *The Loci Technique*
   The loci technique relates to the theory that we may remember more readily if we link what we are learning to things that are native to us, or are already well-established habits. In this technique, you build on the established premise that what is familiar to you has now become a significant part of your working/long-term memory. Those established memories are linked to what you need to learn.

Here are some examples of the loci technique:

✔ *Example one:* One teacher felt that there were five key steps necessary in writing every sentence. She wanted her students to learn these steps:

1. Capital (letter at the beginning of a sentence)
2. Subject
3. Predicate
4. Complete Thought
5. End Mark (punctuation) (Koskovich, 1992 in Jones, 1994)

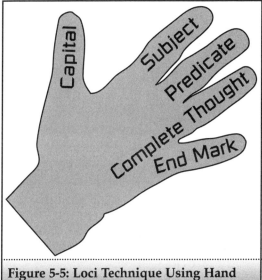

Figure 5-5: Loci Technique Using Hand

The teacher realized that her students always had their hands with them when they wrote a sentence and decided to use each student's hand as a memory tool. She put the five key words on an illustration of a hand and taught her students to visualize the words on their own hands. They could then use this technique to check over the completed sentences to see if they included each key step.

✔ *Example two:* Another teacher recognized that her students studied for tests at home in their bedrooms or in another room. She taught a loci technique using parts of a room to help her students retain information. We already recognize that we can quickly summon up a visual picture of a room we spend a lot of time in. Our brains can readily bring to mind the color of the walls, the type of flooring we have, our bedspread, etc.

A student begins using this strategy by sitting in the room with the information needed to study for a test. The student uses actual furniture in the room as the key points for recall. For example, a student needs to remember the four states that start with A and their capitals (Alaska: Juneau, Arizona: Phoenix, Alabama: Montgomery, Arkansas: Little Rock). The student selects four items in room and then "renames them" with the state and capital. The bed becomes Alaska, the pillows are Juneau, the dresser is Arizona, the drawers are Phoenix, etc. Then the student closes his or her eyes, visualizes each item, and says aloud its new name. The next day when attempting to recall the four states and capitals, the student visualizes his or her room as a starting point and then is able to recall the desired information.

Teacher tips for using the loci technique: Have students use familiar and well-recognized inanimate objects and visuals as links to items that must be learned.

4. *Concept Imagining*

Concept imaging uses exaggeration and visualization to incorporate a concept or an idea. It is most successful when used in teaching content courses such as social studies and science.

The teacher shows students how to make a video or picture in their minds to help them remember concepts, theories, and events. The more exaggerated their videos, the better the recall.

For example, a student needs to remember The Bay of Pigs for a social studies essay test. This event in time occurred during the presidency of John F. Kennedy and involved Fidel Castro, the leader of Cuba. The details of this event are critical to understanding cold war relationships during the 1960s. It is part of most social studies curriculum at middle school and again in high school. To remember this information the student actually visualizes a bay filled with pigs swimming between Florida and Cuba. The visualization is enhanced by adding details such as the people involved, dates, missile sights, and assorted key points that need to be remembered. The student makes the video come to life and encodes it into long-term memory by using exaggerations such as the pigs wearing hats that are stamped with the date when the event occurred. What is the result of this exaggerated visualization technique? When the student practices in this way the brain picks up the novelty and exaggeration allowing better recall of facts and dates because the learning path was so absurd and unique.

Teacher tips for using concept imaging: Have students make exaggerated visualization to represent specific concepts to help them recall the information quickly.

5. *Color*

Color can provide a strong memory cue for long-term recall. The use of color to highlight key words and phrases is helpful for immediate recall and research indicates the brain responds to the uniqueness of color and stimulates recall. In their study of color, researchers Wichmann and colleagues (2002) found color information is stored in the memory and the use of color could increase attention. Their experiments concluded that color-coding is important for rapid identification and recognition.

Have your students color code their notebooks by using one color for each subject and then using those colors as the basis of the notebook (green for science, red for math, etc.). Each subject's file or folder should be in the same color. Write homework assignments and reminders on the board in a specific color of chalk or marker that corresponds to the color coding (science reading assignments or reminders of a science quiz in green).

Here are some ways to "color" your student's memories:

- *Flash cards made with index cards:* Divide topics and items by color (pink for nouns, green for adverbs, etc.).

- *Post-it® Notes:* Use color-coded notes to identify papers that must be returned and as place markers in books.

- *Colored folders:* Keep all papers from one subject in the same colored folder.

- *Pastel lined paper:* Use colored paper for rough drafts, review, and practice. The color adds an additional dimension and focus to your learning activity.

- *Colored tabs on notebook files:* Use tabs to identify subjects by color (green for science, red for math).

Teacher tips for using colors: Color-code subject areas for organization and recall and use color for emphasis and as a focal point to your learning activities.

6. *Mnemonics*

Mnemonics are tricks and devices for improving or increasing memory. One of the leaders in mnemonic research and strategies is Dr. Margo Mastropieri. She has stated, "Research has shown that students who have the most firmly established knowledge base are the ones who can most easily assimilate and apply new information. This phenomenon has been dubbed the 'Matthew effect,' whereby the informationally 'rich' become richer and the informationally 'poor' become poorer" (Mastropieri, 1991).

Mnemonic instruction can be used in content areas such as history and science, to support mathematics concepts and formulas, and to remember rules in reading and spelling. Mnemonics use pictures and auditory clues together. As a result, both auditory and visual learners find them highly successful.

Mnemonics come in an infinite variety. Here are some examples:

- Acronyms (Each letter represents the first letter in a word.)
- Acrostics (A sentence is provided to retrieve letters.)
- Rhyming phrases that have a lively pattern of words
- Peg words (A rhyming system is used for remembering numbers. The numbers are then related, through interactive pictures or images to information associated with numbers.)

You can create your own mnemonics based on the curriculum. You will find that students also enjoy creating their own mnemonic devices. One of my favorite mnemonics is one I created to encourage my students to deploy a variety of strategies when studying for a test. I call it ACE the test (Jones, 1994c). I have the students write the mnemonic on a cue card that they can refer to while they are studying for an exam.

You will ACE the test if you use:
A = ASSOCIATION
C = COLOR
E = EXAGGERATION

Figure 5-6: ACE Mnemonic

Over the years teachers have asked me in workshops for a list of mnemonic cues. The following pages are some of the best ones I have found.

These mnemonics are taken from a wide variety of sources, and I have attempted to list the original source wherever possible. Details can be found in the Resources section at the back of this book.

A note about these mnemonics and mnemonics in general: these devices may not all be considered "politically correct" and should be introduced at your discretion. Because mnemonics work best when they are novel, absurd, and out of the ordinary, they may also not be appropriate for all audiences all the time.

Language Arts

✔ *Store the Story:* Post the following mnemonic cue to help students improve their comprehension skills (Schlegel & Bos, 1986 in Jones, 1994).

S = Setting (Who? What? Where? When?)

T = Trouble (What is the trouble or problem?)

O = Order of events (What happens?)

R = Resolution (What is done to solve the problem?)

E = End (How does the Story end?)

✔ *Read, Cover, Recite, Review:* This mnemonic uses key words to help a student recall a spelling word. First read the word. Then cover it. Finally, recite it aloud and go back later to review the word (Archer, 1988).

✔ *Friend:* An acrostic for remembering how to spell friend:

"Just like the **end** in fri**end**, my fri**end** will be with me until the **end**."

Math

✔ *My Dear Aunt Sally Says:* This is an mnemonic for learning basic math operations (multiply, divide, add, and subtract) (Kilpatrick, 1985).

My	Dear	Aunt	Sally Says
Multiply	Divide	Add	Subtract

✔ *FOIL:* This acronym helps students retrieve the sequence of operations in multiplying two binomials. The product (a = b) (c = d) is the product of the **F**irst items (ac), the **O**uter terms (ad), the **I**nner terms (bc) and the **L**ast terms (bd) (Kilpatrick, 1985).

Music

✔ *Every Good Boy Deserves Fudge:* This is an acrostic denoting the notes on the lines of the treble clef (EGBDF).

✔ *STAB:* This acronym names the four voices in a quartet. The visual cue is to picture someone going to stab a quartet as it is singing (Lorayne & Lucas, 1974).

S oprano

T enor

A lto

B ass (or Baritone)

Science/Social Studies

✔ *My Very Educated Mother Just Served Us Nine Pizzas:* An acrostic for remembering the nine planets in order: Mercury, Venus, Earth, Mars, Jupiter, Saturn, Uranus, Neptune, and Pluto.

✔ *Liquid, solid, gas — if I remember this, I will pass:* This rhyming phrase helps students remember the three states of matter.

✔ *Welcome to FARM-B:* This acrostic helps students remember the types of vertebrates.

F ish

A mphibians

R eptiles

M ammals

B irds

✔ *King Phillip Chases Old Fat Girl Scouts:* This mnemonic helps students remember the elements of the Linneus Classification System in hierarchical order. The beginning letters of the words in the sentence are the beginning letters of the following: Kingdom, Phylum, Class, Order, Family, Genus, and Species.

✔ *Roy G. Biv:* This acronym helps students recall the colors of the visible light spectrum in order:

Red Orange Yellow Green Blue Indigo Violet

✔ *Never Eat Shredded Wheat:* A mnemonic to remember the four cardinal directions:

Never	**Eat**	**Shredded**	**Wheat**
North	**East**	**South**	**West**

✔ *HOMES:* An acronym for remembering the names of the Great Lakes. Each letter in the word HOMES stands for the first letter of one of the five Great Lakes:

H uron

O ntario

M ichigan

E rie

S uperior

Dr. Mastropieri cautions teachers that to teach a mnemonic device successfully they must first actually show and incorporate the mnemonic in their instruction. This way the students see it actually working in the lesson. Her research maintains that in a decade of studies, students who received mnemonic instruction greatly outperformed control groups taught by traditional instructional techniques. She encourages attributing student's success in learning with the use of mnemonic strategies. In addition to teaching specific mnemonics, encourage your entire class to create their own devices for a lesson. Have students share mnemonics they have used with the rest of the class.

Possible Causes of Memory Loss

It would be ineffective for our brains to maintain every fragment of information we are exposed to throughout life, and you experience memory changes over the course of your life. Your brain's operations fluctuate and will respond to multiple environmental factors, including the condition of your emotional state, stress, possible injury, and different insight and genetic factors. You will be subjected to changes in your memory in both the areas of input and output.

The influence of stress can be critical to memory pathways. Researchers have demonstrated that the brain releases the chemical **cortisol** during stress. It affects encoding and breaks down connections; thus, we lose valuable memories and perhaps the ability to quickly recall key pieces of information. (Chapter 8 contains further information about the effects of stress on the brain and memory.) A serious injury to the brain such as an accident, trauma, or a stroke can alter brain pathways. This alteration of function can result in lost memories or connections. Some syndrome disorders can also have an affect on brain activity. It is speculated that persons diagnosed with attention deficit disorder, for example, have weaker short-term memory based on recent PET scans indicating weaker brain activity in the front right cortex. This influences the output of short-term memory and creates a "Now I have it, now I don't" response for these people. Aging also plays a large part in brain activity. The aging female may experience estrogen loss as a part of natural aging process, and this loss of estrogen — a key chemical in supporting memory process — results in memory confusion and loss. Finally, it is noted that people who are depressed have irregular levels of serotonin

Factors Contributing to Memory Loss
• Stress
• Menopausal symptoms
• Possible Alzheimer's
• Medications, including drugs for anxiety, antidepressants, high blood pressure and insulin
• Attention Deficit/Hyperactivity Disorder
• Injury to frontal lobe
• Confusion related to stroke
• Dysfunctional thyroid gland
• Depression (affects short-term memory)
• Regular marijuana or alcohol use

Figure 5-7: Normal Causes for Memory Loss

and will be forgetful as well as being down or sad. Figure 5-7 lists reasons why a person's memory capacity may be reduced.

Encouraging Memory

There are many ways to incorporate memory-building skills into our lives and the lives of the students we influence on a daily basis. Every day the classroom provides mental exercise, which is critical to the developing brain. Intellectually stimulating games, problem-solving activities, and active interaction with discussion and debate will strengthen elaborative encoding and brain cell networks. Students who pursue higher formal education and continue to participate in ongoing learning experiences throughout their adult lives will benefit from the brain creating a "neural reserve" of denser, stronger nerve/cell connections (Patoine, 2001). See Figure 5-8 on the following page for tips on improving memory.

Improving the Quality of Memory

- **Physical activity:** Provide physical activity opportunities throughout the school day. Regular exercise will hone memory skills. Look at resources like *Brain Gym*[1] for brief exercises you can employ with students during the day.

- **Reduce stress:** Model ways for students to reduce stress and manage relaxation. Demonstrate deep breathing and counting to ten to show students how to take time to relax their minds before a test. Teach visualization skills and positive mind focus.

- **Get organized:** Help students learn to organize their lifestyle. Teach daily planning, use of organizers, and inexpensive ways to store and organize their materials. Teach color-coding as a tool students can employ in many ways in their school and home life. Provide a classroom environment that is a model for organizational strategies.

- **Put it in writing:** Teach students to write down what they are trying to remember. Encourage them to use Post-it® notes, note pads, calendars, and day planners. Teach them how to use computer-generated calendars and schedule guides.

- **Use visualization:** Show students how to make a mental visual image of something they want to remember. Teach them to take a picture with the "camera in their brain."

- **Teach memory strategies:** Employ memory strategies in your daily lesson plan. Demonstrate how students can commit to memory what you are teaching. Use mnemonics, patterns, and visual clues to enhance student's memory experiences.

- **Monitor student strategies:** Ask students to demonstrate how they study for a test and prepare for a long-term assignment. Have them model their own personal memory techniques.

- **Provide rehearsal and practice for test taking:** Have students practice working with multiple choice format questions. Give them opportunities to time themselves accomplishing different tasks (i.e., time how long it takes to tie shoes, write name and address, walk from front door of school to back door) so they feel more comfortable when placed in a timed standardized testing situation.

Figure 5-8: Tips for Improving Memory in the Classroom

[1]See the Resources section for more information on *Brain Gym.*

> Life is a succession of lessons,
> which must be lived to be understood.
>
> —*Ralph Waldo Emerson*

6 Cognition: The Brain's Room

In Chapter 1, I described the teacher as the "environmental engineer" in the classroom. To me, this means the teacher is in charge of students' learning opportunities and the place and time where those opportunities will be delivered. The environmental engineer understands how you learn best and makes sure sometime during the day opportunities are available for you to take advantage of your learning strength. Classrooms today contain a diverse palette of learners. A teacher cannot stop and offer one thing to one child and then move and offer another technique to another child. A teacher who attempted such an approach would soon burn out. Rather, master teachers will incorporate a cluster of good teaching tools and materials that will help all children.

Working with Diverse Learners

Raul struggled with reading, and now at 8th grade he is still reading at about one grade below level. He has been in resource room since second grade and soon may not receive services because of his improvement. He is well behaved and a hard worker, but lately his parents report he is "losing his self esteem." They report that even though he has made tremendous strides, he notes he cannot read as well as others at his grade level, and he compares himself to them daily. His creativity is widely observed both at home and at school. For example, he makes things out of discarded trash items and has gained considerable expertise with a number of tools and specific woodworking equipment. His teacher understands his limits but is looking for multiple ways to help him succeed.

Raul's teacher can use her expertise as an environmental engineer and manipulate the surroundings to make sure there are times during the day when Raul's strengths will be of great use. By recognizing his learning style and personal strengths the teacher can focus more on what Raul *does* do, not what he *doesn't* do. The teacher can make Raul feel more secure in the classroom by offering a climate where he eventually sees what he does well and how it contributes to the success of the class.

The following sections illustrate ways to use the information we have been learning about sensory partiality, multiple learning styles, and brain-based research to create a productive environment within your classroom:

A Routine Setting

Research indicates that our brains require and need structure and an organized format in which to maintain, learn, and grow. You can meet this need by offering daily schedules that are well-marked, consistent, and follow a curriculum plan. Here are some things to keep in mind:

- *Post the schedule for each day:* Make the schedule accessible for all to see. If changes occur in your plan, alert children well before they happen. Speak positively and confidently as you discuss the changes.

- *Clearly mark accomplished activities:* After each activity is completed, have a student helper remove the item from the schedule. This can be done by erasing, crossing off, or simply checking. This crossing off is critical. Research indicates students feel more secure and aware in the class when they know what they have accomplished so far.

- *Use rituals:* Rituals are an important part of the classroom environment. Eric Jensen, author of *Teaching with the Brain in Mind* (1998), maintains that rituals are simple, repetitive acts that become predictable. Rituals build security with their predictability. When a student knows there will be a schedule on the wall of the room at the beginning of every day, it creates confidence and a sense of expectation. It allows the student the reassurance of a plan. The student will know where to look and how to respond to what is happening today. Rituals are important because they free up the mind for doing other things. Because we can count on rituals for organizing and handling our daily routines, our brains will be more ready for learning. We generally feel comforted and more protected in a learning environment that offers rituals. Marilee B. Sprenger (2002) writes, "Classrooms need many rituals to provide this feeling of security, which may help de-stress the students" (p. 38).

The most employed ritual in a classroom is the actual agenda or routine of planning the total day with students. You might do a webbing activity, such as the one shown in Figure 6-1 to plan the day with your students. Your daily plan needs to be structured well in advance and designed to promote times for optimum learning based on biological information about learning (see Figure 3-2 on page 34). The time spent on activities could be arranged based on how long students can stay focused on direct instruction and how long they can maintain focus in dispersed activity group work. Set up your day knowing that students will remember best the information that comes first. They will remember second best the final information you give them.

Typical lengths of time to be considered include taking the age of the student and attributing one minute of concentration to each year. For example, a seven-year-old can stay focused for seven minutes on a particular task. This span of time increases one minute for each year of age to a maximum of around 20-25 minutes. These times are presented as guidelines only — all children vary in their attention spans. Many factors will affect how well a child can participate in an activity: the type of activity, the prior learning experience, what has preceded the activity throughout the student's day, and the student's level of interest in the task.

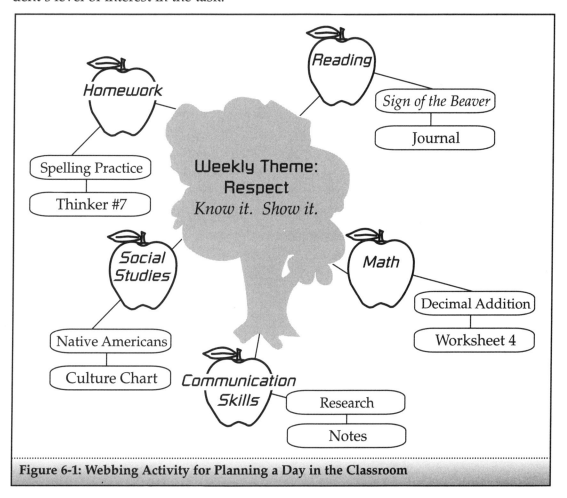

Figure 6-1: Webbing Activity for Planning a Day in the Classroom

The following pages illustrate suggestions for a well-managed day and a well-managed class session with a focus of taking advantage of appropriate blocks of time for optimum performance. The plan also includes how to integrate many of the brain-based theories into a typical day.

A Well-Planned Day: Elementary School

Greeting students at door: This welcome at the door helps the teacher connect with an immediate impression and provides for a visual barometer of students' possible moods and attitudes. It creates ritual and connection. This connection can help you set the climate for the day in your room.

Activities on desk to do as students arrive: The teacher places an individual review lesson at each student's place each morning. This may be a math game to review or reinforce a new concept, a puzzle, or a vocabulary-building game. This gives the student time to work on an activity of high interest as the class slowly transitions from unstructured to more highly-structured activities.

Morning meeting: Start the morning with a musical piece or song that students recognize and alerts them to the fact that the day is starting. Following this song, daily rituals begin. Daily classroom organizational activities (lunch count, attendance, collecting of fees, daily announcements, and review of helpers) are accomplished during this time period.

Morning charge: Present songs, poems, and inspirational messages to inspire the emotional side of the brain and set up the plan for the day.

Review of the daily plan: Web a daily lesson plan on the board for all to see and review (see Figure 6-1 on page 77). The daily plan is color-coded by subject area. Homework captains collect papers and inform the teacher of any missing items.

Transition: This critical strategy offers an activity that helps students move easily from one activity to another. Review the first item of the daily plan on the board and guide the students into the first academic period.

First academic period: Instruction planned by the teacher begins. Place the most essential material at the beginning of the lesson. At the end of this period there is a gradual wind down and transition activity that flows to the next period. Brief group activity or working with peers and tutors can follow each instructional period. At the end of the period use your overhead to highlight and review key information as you exit the lesson.

Second academic period: instruction as above

Break/Recess/Brain gymnastics

Third academic period: instruction as above

Lunch

Transition time: Again, plan an organized passage of time, offering activities to take students from the unstructured lunch to a slightly more structured activity, followed by a more structured formal learning experience.

Fourth academic period: instruction as above

Break/Recess/Brain exercises

Fifth academic period: instruction as above

Wind down and Review of the day: Review of the day can include the information students learned that day for the first time, what students enjoyed most in the day, what they thought was fun, what activity they participated in that they felt they did their very best at, plans for tomorrow, etc.

Recording of assignments/ homework: This time period allows partners to check one another's books and assignments before leaving.

Exit: The teacher selects a different student each afternoon to stand at the door, say goodbye, and shake hands. The teacher designates this student as the "Celebrity" at the door. As the student handles this culminating activity, the teacher can hand out reminder stickers (colored dots corresponding to subject areas on students' assignment notebooks) as cues for information they need for the next day. These colored dot stickers are helpful memory prompts for students who need additional cueing for recall. For example, a red dot on an assignment book is a reminder of a math test tomorrow.

A Well-Planned Single Class Session

Greeting on entering

Unstructured activity slowly leads to more structured activity

Review of yesterday's lessons

Recording of assignments and homework retrieval

Lesson: Start with key information and the basic skill you are teaching. Use a motivator right from the start. Remember, the first 15 minutes is when your students' focus is at its best.

Application: Move to class and individual practice and feedback. Students work alone or in small groups on the daily lesson.

Review of lesson: Wrap up the session with a review of key points.

Exit: Celebrity of the day says good-bye to everyone at the door.

Flexible Seating Arrangements

The information regarding brain chemistry indicates that as a person learns new information it is critical that the learning environment remain interactive and provides both novelty and routine. As we learned in Chapter 3, we should not change the location of a student's seat prior to a test. However, once you are ready to embark on a *new* learning activity, a change of seat can add variety and interest for the brain. Remember, though, that seating arrangements should not be changed without prior notice. Many students need an opportunity to process what is going to happen before you change their location. Highly distracted students, such as those diagnosed with Attention Deficit Disorder or Attention Deficit Hyperactivity Disorder (ADD/ADHD), should benefit from preferential seating whenever you change arrangements. They need to have a direct view of you from any seat and do not do well placed near very active centers like the door or a pencil sharpener. Research indicates (1994) that students with ADD/ADHD are twice as likely to be disruptive sitting in a group or cluster situation. The U shape is a highly regarded seating arrangement for all students, and the child with ADD/ADHD particularly benefits from this configuration. They profit from the U shape because it offers a direct line of interaction with the teacher and little distraction from others. Figure 6-2 illustrates some successful seating arrangements for the classroom.

The Physical Seat

The plastic molded seat that so many schools now have can be uncomfortable to students after just a brief time using it. Allow students to bring in cushions or chair pillows to make their seats more comfortable. Research indicates students will be more focused when they are able to feel physically at ease and relaxed. Some very active students prefer sitting on a large activity ball rather than a chair at times. Others are successful sitting "cowboy style" on the chair with the front part of the seat providing a secure base.

Children under the age of seven benefit from doing puzzles and motor activities while they lie on their tummies with hands outstretched.

Greetings

Here is the way to start the day positively and a way to assure direct student contact. When the bell rings, be at the door and greet the students as they enter. If you can manage it, do the same as they exit. This is your time to give each student a personal hello and eye contact. It starts each day and session with a clean slate, and it offers a ritual that students thrive on. Because exit time may be busier than entrance time, try this strategy for the end of a class period or day: at the end of the class or session, choose a different class member who stands at the door and shakes hands with fellow students as they exit. Prior to the bell ringing for the period or day, have the board helper read the name of the

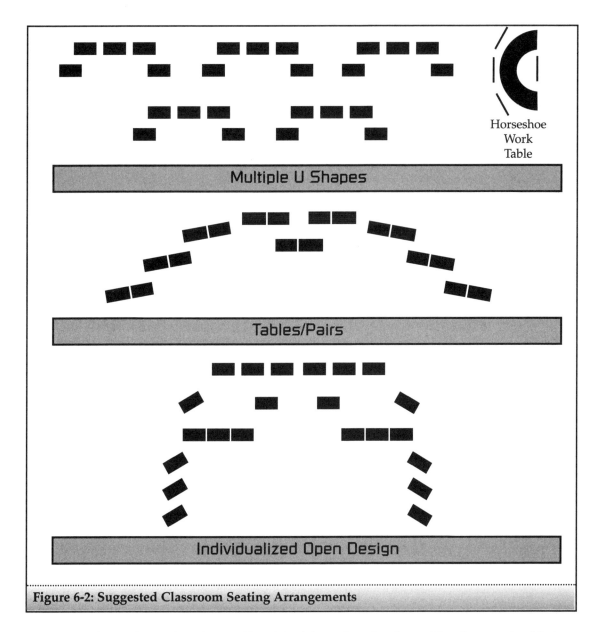

Figure 6-2: Suggested Classroom Seating Arrangements

student who is that day's official "celebrity" at the door. Use the word *celebrity* to make the job seem fun and special for students. Humor and good spirit are motivating to the brain. I found greeting my students at the door very rewarding but particularly gratifying when I taught at middle school. Brain research indicates this age range will be experiencing some difficult social fluctuation as the brain slowly formulates social maturation. Sometimes just a look in the eye of a particular student let me know what kind of day I had ahead of me and what I'd better prepare for! It seemed to be a perfect way to attempt to read my students' moods for the day.

Using Language to Encourage the Brain

Incorporate a positive tone in your language to encourage modeling and develop an expanding attitude about language in your students' minds. Select key phrases that will enable your students to make the most of their own language skills and adapt to their understanding of verbal context.

To develop a team spirit at the elementary level, try referring to your students as "friends," "teams," or "partners." Use these positive image words instead of the more commonly heard "you guys," "kids," and "class." Which of the following sounds better to you?

- "Friends, please line up now to get ready for lunch."
- "You guys need to line up now."

Some other positive things to say include, "Friends, I need your attention now" and "Check to see if your friend is ready to go to the library now."

> "Your language can guide students in their goal-setting and in planning a positive direction for action."

Your language can guide students in their goal-setting and in planning a positive direction for action. The statement, "It's great to know" can be used in many ways. For example, you might say, "It's great to know that you are getting your things ready to go home." The addition of this simple phrase sends a positive modeling message, rather than, "Are you ready yet?" You can also say, "It's great to know that you will take turns on the equipment when we go to the playground," instead of, "You had difficulty yesterday taking turns; you'd better watch it today." This phrase can subtly cue a student about how their own responses can be phrased in a positive way. You can also interchange "It's great to know" with the words "It makes me happy to see." For example, you can say, "It makes me happy to see table three ready to go to lunch so quickly," instead of, "How long must we wait for table three?"

Brain research indicates that we can encode positive behavior changes for students by using mental pictures and linguistic information that guide behaviors in a meaningful, proactive way. Another way to use language in an inspirational context is to use brief, enthusiastic statements. Try using brief cheers or chants to stimulate mental stamina and create positive spirit. Here are some examples:

- *Reminder for homework*
  Homework, Homework, That's our clue,
  I can remember it,
  Can you?

- *Call for line up*

  1, 2, 3 — 1, 2, 3, — 1, 2, 3, 4, 5, 6!

  1, 2, 3 — 1, 2, 3, — 1, 2, 3, 4, 5, 6!

  Line up!

- *Class Cheer*

  This class has spirit,

  Yes, we do,

  I can do it,

  So can you!

- *Birthday Cheer*

  It's your birthday,

  We can see,

  Happy Birthday,

  From the class and me!

- *The Wave*

  Cut out large hand patterns and staple them to tongue depressors. Give every student one "hand" to keep in his or her desk. When someone needs a special "salute" for good behavior or congratulations for an accomplishment, say to the class, "Let's all give Jack a wave for his great work on that book report." Students pull out their hands and wave at the honored student.

Class Posters

Have students design motivating posters to place in the room for visual stimulus. Choose dynamic slogans and change the posters regularly to provide continual variety and motivation. Here are some suggested slogans for class posters:

- This Class Can!
- This Class Tries!
- We Do Succeed!
- Rise Above!
- Look Ahead!
- I Can Turn That Into "Yes"!

Add Variety to Routine

Select daily routines and add some variety or brevity to their presentation. This change will keep the brain interested and avoid cognitive fatigue that occurs with repetitive activities. It is often during these "rote" procedures when restless and difficult behavior arises, so do your best to offer a change to keep students interested. David Sousa (2001a) warns to avoid predictable patterns when calling on students, such as alphabetical order, up and down rows, or raised hands. He believes these patterns signal the students when they will be held accountable, thereby allowing them to go off task before and after their turns.

Here are some ways you can offer variety and eliminate rote procedures within your day.

- *Activity count-off:* Avoid counting off by number; instead, offer two well-known names or groupings to be counted as pairs. Here are some pairs to consider:
  - ✔ Batman and Robin
  - ✔ Salt and Pepper
  - ✔ Bush and Cheney
  - ✔ Milk and Cookies
  - ✔ Mickey and Minnie

- *Birthday division:* When students need to work together in groups, divide them by their birthdays. Group students whose birthdays fall in the same season. This grouping by birthdays always seems to create a certain instant spirit of camaraderie among your students. For example, Team A is made up of students whose birthdays are in the fall (September, October, November). You will probably observe that this technique develops a feeling of connectedness among students.

Following are a number of activities and ideas to add interest and variety to your classroom environment and daily routines:

- *Coach's corner:* When you arrange your classroom, provide one small U-shaped table in the room for small group and instructional work. At times "advertise" that you will be offering extra practice at this table for students who need additional assistance on a smaller scale. Call the table the "Coach's Corner" or name it after yourself ("Miss Brown's Coaching Corner). The space can be used by paraprofessionals, teachers of related support services, tutors, and student teachers. Tell students, "if you don't understand, please join a coach for extra practice." After any lesson, invite a student who particularly seems to understand what was taught, to be a guest coach and offer additional assistance to his or her peers.

- *Call for line up*
  1, 2, 3 — 1, 2, 3, — 1, 2, 3, 4, 5, 6!
  1, 2, 3 — 1, 2, 3, — 1, 2, 3, 4, 5, 6!
  Line up!

- *Class Cheer*
  This class has spirit,
  Yes, we do,
  I can do it,
  So can you!

- *Birthday Cheer*
  It's your birthday,
  We can see,
  Happy Birthday,
  From the class and me!

- *The Wave*
  Cut out large hand patterns and staple them to tongue depressors. Give every student one "hand" to keep in his or her desk. When someone needs a special "salute" for good behavior or congratulations for an accomplishment, say to the class, "Let's all give Jack a wave for his great work on that book report." Students pull out their hands and wave at the honored student.

Class Posters

Have students design motivating posters to place in the room for visual stimulus. Choose dynamic slogans and change the posters regularly to provide continual variety and motivation. Here are some suggested slogans for class posters:
- This Class Can!
- This Class Tries!
- We Do Succeed!
- Rise Above!
- Look Ahead!
- I Can Turn That Into "Yes"!

Add Variety to Routine

Select daily routines and add some variety or brevity to their presentation. This change will keep the brain interested and avoid cognitive fatigue that occurs with repetitive activities. It is often during these "rote" procedures when restless and difficult behavior arises, so do your best to offer a change to keep students interested. David Sousa (2001a) warns to avoid predictable patterns when calling on students, such as alphabetical order, up and down rows, or raised hands. He believes these patterns signal the students when they will be held accountable, thereby allowing them to go off task before and after their turns.

Here are some ways you can offer variety and eliminate rote procedures within your day.

- *Activity count-off:* Avoid counting off by number; instead, offer two well-known names or groupings to be counted as pairs. Here are some pairs to consider:
  - ✔ Batman and Robin
  - ✔ Salt and Pepper
  - ✔ Bush and Cheney
  - ✔ Milk and Cookies
  - ✔ Mickey and Minnie

- *Birthday division:* When students need to work together in groups, divide them by their birthdays. Group students whose birthdays fall in the same season. This grouping by birthdays always seems to create a certain instant spirit of camaraderie among your students. For example, Team A is made up of students whose birthdays are in the fall (September, October, November). You will probably observe that this technique develops a feeling of connectedness among students.

Following are a number of activities and ideas to add interest and variety to your classroom environment and daily routines:

- *Coach's corner:* When you arrange your classroom, provide one small U-shaped table in the room for small group and instructional work. At times "advertise" that you will be offering extra practice at this table for students who need additional assistance on a smaller scale. Call the table the "Coach's Corner" or name it after yourself ("Miss Brown's Coaching Corner). The space can be used by paraprofessionals, teachers of related support services, tutors, and student teachers. Tell students, "if you don't understand, please join a coach for extra practice." After any lesson, invite a student who particularly seems to understand what was taught, to be a guest coach and offer additional assistance to his or her peers.

- *Sign in, please:* If you teach or instruct a small class session or therapy session, you will want to offer an additional tool along with your daily greeting. Have a sign-in board where each student leaves an "autograph" when entering and erases it when leaving. Tell students to write their names the way they will when they are famous some day. Label the board, "Our Autographs Book." Provide a sparkle pen or unusually-colored pen for students to sign with. This simple task offers a ritual upon entering a small, different situation and provides immediate structure in what can be perceived by some students as a less-structured situation. This small activity offers discipline and routine to your session.

- *Bulletin boards that teach:* Imagine your bulletin board as a teacher on the wall! Make the material there meaningful and memorable. Focus on key instructional cues that students need to learn. You will have many students staring at it during the course of the day; therefore, your bulletin board should teach or review something that is critical to the learning environment.

- *Hands-on manipulatives:* Provide well-organized objects in containers to be used for multiple activities. Fill containers with buttons, chips, noodles, bottle caps, cubes, plastic balls, tubes, paper clips, straws, etc. All of these can be used for hands-on activities and can demonstrate sorting, categorization, counting, estimation, and numerous other activities. Organize the materials in margarine tubs or other small containers and label them well. Use color-coding to organize by group (types of foods in pink, fasteners in green, etc.). These materials will always be at hand for counting activities, estimation, and visualization.

- *Privacy and "chill out" corners:* Offer comfort zones in your room. These include quiet places with pillows, rugs, and soft chairs. Provide students with a CD player and headphones for listening to soft music from Brahms to New Wave to Joshua Redmond and Kenny G. These special places are where active brains can enjoy some down time to recharge and revitalize.

- *Self-controlled and guided responsibility areas:* There are many rituals that go on in a class every day. These rituals range from attendance to collecting lunch money and from ordering books to signing up for a field trip. These activities may include recording of daily weather, lunch count, opinion polls, etc. Equip your room with predictable charts, graphs, and signs to help coordinate these activities and allow for maximum student participation. Research indicates that students felt more secure and felt they had accomplished more when they were able to cross off or erase on a schedule that they had completed a task. If you find yourself handing back papers, passing books out, and erasing the board — STOP! Turn these activities into student-directed activities. A student should do every routine job in the classroom. This promotes responsibility and encourages students to feel they are important members of the class.

- *Tracking classroom accomplishments:* On your daily plan, which is posted in room, provide a system to remove each completed task from the plan as it is finished. To accomplish this try the following:

  1. When an activity is finished, have a student erase or check off the activity on the daily plan. Give this responsibility to a different student every day.

  2. Place a daily schedule on a pocket planner chart with each activity on a sentence strip. As you accomplish each activity, turn the sentence strip over.

  3. Take time at end of each planned activity to have students take out markers and cross off what they have done on their individual assignment books, calendars, or day planners.

- *Tracking group work accomplishments:* Try this for centers or group work activities.

  1. Place a clipboard with an attached pencil and a list of class members' names at each work center.

  2. Have children cross off their own names when they finish working at the center.

Instead of individual lists, you might make a card for each student that contains a list of all the work centers. A student then finds her or his card and marks off the center just completed. Identify the card to students as their "What a Kid List" (Jones 1995).

The goal is to complete all free time activities on the card and to keep a record of that on their own. As students complete activities on the "What a Kid List" card, they cross off the task. At the end of the center session, students hand in their completed cards so the teacher can review what they have done. The teacher can give points for completed tasks and points can be traded for class privileges, homework passes, and additional free time.

Increasing Comprehension

A recent study suggests that comprehension increases when the following steps are followed (Crowley & Siegler, 1999):

1. Students receive a visual demonstration of a task to be learned.
2. Students hear a verbal explanation of the task from another person
3. The information is then cemented with a reiteration of the technique in the learner's own words.

The following strategies support the above procedure:

- *Tutor centers:* Provide a corner of the room or a specially-marked area in your school where volunteers, grandparents, and parents can offer additional tutoring, mentoring, and coaching. As a teacher, I looked around my school for these available nooks and crannies in my building and found places under the stairs, a cloakroom, and even behind a hall trophy case. I borrowed chairs from the assembly storage room and placed a large paper grocery bag over the back of each on which I wrote, "Reserved for Room 5 tutorial help." I took large potato chip cans and filled them with extra equipment such as paper, pencils, stapler, crayons, etc., for the volunteers' use. I took a moveable cart and filled it with extra games, books, a tape recorder, and other extra materials I had. When tutors came to work they could sign in on the cart's clipboard and remove any materials they wanted to work with. I left the cart outside of my room so tutors could come and go as they pleased on the days they were helping. I could also use this cart to post special messages to the tutors, such as information regarding specific students.

- *Kids teaching kids:* Your room is your student's community. They spend the bulk of every day there. You can help students use active participation within this learning environment. Students remember more when they can interact, work, talk, and plan with the information they are learning. Research indicates that the average retention rate after 24 hours is highest when the student has engaged in the practice of teaching others and immediately putting to use what they have learned. Allow times for group work, partner work, and one-to-one interaction to maximize this opportunity to teach the material to one another.

  Set up times where students teach one another. Label this time on your daily plan as "Kids Teach" or "Time to Teach a Friend" and have students review something you have taught with a friend and classmate. Designate a specific time for this interaction to occur. Try to schedule this time to follow when you have just introduced new material. Allow students a brief time to review their notes, the handout, or the book that was used, and then have them meet in pairs. Assign pairs initially so no one feels slighted or left out. Tell the pairs they have five minutes to review and teach each other the new concept. This activity stimulates recall and encourages socialization. The next activity outlines another way to use this technique.

- *Teaching assistant chair:* This approach allows students to have specific review on a task, but it allows them to feel they are not being singled out. Place two chairs marked "1" and "2" to the side of the room. Have two students sit facing one another on these chairs and drill one another on a specific task or set of information. For example, the student in chair 1 asks the student in chair 2 to spell the words for this week's vocabulary list. The student in chair 1 corrects the word if the other student spells it incorrectly and acknowledges a correctly spelled word. After a designated period of time, the students switch chairs and reverse roles. This technique gives weaker students a chance to feel in control yet still review information that they are having trouble with.

- *The waiting chair:* Place a comfortable chair by your desk or workstation. This chair is for students wanting to talk with you on an individual basis. There are times during the day when students are working independently and you are seated or working throughout the room. Students who want to have an individual session with you go to this chair and wait until you are available. This avoids having students standing or waiting by your desk in lines and wasting time away from their own work. They can look up and see if the chair is occupied or not.

- *Koosh® ball catch:* Use a brightly colored Koosh® ball to help out during feedback and question and answer time. When you call on students, throw them the ball and have them hold it as they answer. This helps students stay focused on who is speaking and adds an element of variety to a feedback session.

Musical Accompaniment

There is a strong movement in the field of music education to include music as a critical part of every child's day. This movement became prominent in the late 1990s, when the College Entrance Exam Service board studied the students who took the SAT in 1996. They found that students who sang or played an instrument scored 51 points higher on the verbal section and 39 points higher on the math section than those students who did not. Additional researchers studying music noted the brain's response to pattern and rhythm. This influx of information about the power of music influenced one state, Georgia, to respond by giving every newborn baby in the state a CD of classical music. The goal was that new parents play would this music immediately for their infant in hopes of stimulating intellectual growth. Although this early research is promising and

exciting, we still don't have concrete results from this type of study that says, "Play a CD of Chopin music for fifteen minutes a day and you will be at the top of your class."

> "... music can create a climate, influence a mood, and possibly ... provide a stress-reducing effect."

What we can garner from this research is that music can create a climate, influence a mood, and possibly its beat or pattern can provide a stress-reducing effect. Some teachers believe that in a busy classroom, music may indeed offer a positive and tranquil respite from the daily grind. Is there a particular type of music that will be more successful than another? At this point it seems to be more a function of the music's rhythm or beat that seems inspirational or capable of influencing change. Some students respond well to the addition of a musical background as they work, while others may view it as an intrusion. Some very distracted ADD/ADHD students maintain that one sound on in the room helps them focus more on what they are doing. Others feel that earplugs helped them tune out irritating sounds and that they were able to internalize more when they wore ear plugs for independent study.

At any rate, music is certainly something you can easily introduce to your classroom and then observe the class's responses yourself. Most teachers who use music choose instrumentals and music that has a strong, repetitive beat. Offer students the choice of music with or without earphones. The Brain Store catalog mentioned in the Resource section has many musical selections designed for typical classroom activities.

Classroom Considerations

The following suggestions relate to the the equipment in and physical considerations of the classroom and how they relate to cognition and addressing various learning styles:

- *Resource materials:* The teacher who uses the entire class environment as a way to invigorate and excite learning needs to collect a variety of tools to achieve this. Technology has produced many exciting pieces of equipment to enhance our learning environment, but some of the standard pieces of equipment that you may find in storage in your school are also helpful. Although these items might not be quite as up-to-date as something new, they are valuable for one-on-one instruction and can add a unique application to a learning experience. These pieces of equipment include older computers, tape recorders, calculators, overheads, typewriters, Language Masters, speed readers, small hand-held slide viewers, filmstrip projectors, etc. Have these things available on an as-needed basis in your room for students to work with for review and creative instruction.

- *Take-home centers:* As a teacher, I often had materials that were donated or left over in my room. I also learned to collect "freebies" such as handouts from museums, utility companies' free educational materials, samples from educational warehouses, discards from stationary stores, printing company samples, and thrift store items. As I collected these materials I would place them in clean, donated fried chicken buckets. I labeled the buckets "Brainstorming Buckets" and any child in the class (or school for that matter) could take one home to keep. Other items to put in the buckets include old paperbacks, videotapes, desk equipment, used and outdated textbooks, catalogs, and old tapes. Having these materials available is one way to continually add variety to education and to make learning an ongoing activity. To encourage continual learning outside of the classroom, send these extra materials home on an as-needed basis. Students can use the materials at home and include their parents and family members in their educational experiences. At the elementary level use boxes or buckets as containers for the material. At the middle school level, place materials in colorful plastic legal-sized envelopes.

- *Organization Center:* Recognize that your students look to you for guidance and inspiration. Create a room designed for optimal learning that is systematic and well organized. Here are some ways to reduce distractions and increase organization:

  ✔ Color code and label materials by subject and interest area.

  ✔ Put similar storage containers together and organize them by color and shape.

  ✔ Keep unused materials out of sight and in storage. Bring out only what you need.

  ✔ Post schedules and lists of where materials and items are kept and stored.

  ✔ Label closets, drawers, and shelves as to their contents.

  ✔ Use discarded video boxes as holders for small pencils, erasers, and personal items.

- *Board work:* Be aware that students with learning disabilities and attention disorders may have difficulty copying from the board onto their papers. They may have a problem with vision impairment or visual motor memory integration. Visual motor memory integration difficulty indicates the student will have poor recall for what they are trying to copy and place on paper. Their challenge is remembering what they have just seen and writing it. Therefore, it takes them longer to copy from the board or from book to paper. Some ways to support these students are listed on the next page:

✔ When you put material on the board use careful, neat printing or well-spaced cursive. Use cursive only if you are sure students can read it. Many students today are not using cursive and may not be able to read it. (Note: In this millennium, cursive is becoming a lost art form. The computer encourages printing and all forms and applications today require it. Have you ever seen a form that says "Please use cursive"?)

✔ To support students' recall for what they are copying, add visual dimensions to the work. Place a block around specific areas you have written and highlight the outside of the block in one color so students know where to look. Cover busy areas on boards so students are directed to the area they should be looking at.

✔ Number anything you place on the board to increase visual support for copying. If the amount of text is lengthy, add boxes, lines, arrows, or circles around words in the material. This random placing insures that a child who is not committing words to memory is still able to copy from the board in a word to word fashion. The shapes, boxes, and arrows serve as visual cues.

✔ Have a student read the material you put on the board aloud to the class before you discuss it.

✔ Make copies of outlines you intend to put on the board, display on an overhead, or show in a Power Point presentation. Give copies to students whose 504 plan or IEP requires their own copy of notes.

Rewards and Reinforcements

Everyone needs reward and encouragement to succeed. The brain will respond to different reinforcement by literally activating the neurotransmitter serotonin so we feel physical pleasure with the emotional response. Here are some great ways to help students feel appreciated in the classroom:

• *Pat on the back award:* Draw a hand on a colored sheet of paper. Make multiple copies. Write on the hand, "You deserve a pat on the back for your hard work." Present these awards to individual students several times a week when you spot a special behavior.

• *Bird notes:* Place a small tree branch in a container in the room. Make colorful bird cutouts with a string attached to each one. Write on the bird, "A little bird told me you were so . . . ." Fill in the dots with a positive behavior you observed. Present to a student when you see a positive behavior. The student writes his or her name on the bird and hangs it from the tree branch.

- *Pot o' gold:* Fill an empty bucket with little prizes such as new pencils, colorful pens, erasers, and key chains. When you spot a student doing something "above and beyond normal behavior," hold up the bucket and state, "Friends, I just saw Justin helping our student teacher locate materials. I have to pass him the bucket for that." The bucket is passed and the student removes a token.

- *Chair for a day:* Make colorful tags with one of the following words printed on each one: *respectful, happy, friendly, good humor, kind, caring, sharing, generous, careful, on task,* and *thoughtful.* When you observe a student performing one of the behaviors, place that tag around the back of his or her chair. It remains there for the day.

- *Bucket brigade for free time:* The research on the brain indicates that it responds well to and seeks out novelty and variety. Within your daily plan, there will be times when some students are completed with work and others are still working. These "down" periods require planning to provide some stimulus for students who are finished and waiting. Provide activities for free time when students are finished with their daily work that are unique and foster creative, inventive thought. Purchase large colorful buckets and fill them with theme-based activities. Create the contents of the buckets around a theme. This theme will support the student's desire to explore and know more about the particular topic. Label and color the buckets by theme and place specific items in each bucket that enhance that theme.

  Here are some examples of theme buckets:
  - ✔ **Math bucket:** Fill the bucket with accounting pads, calculators with mounted adding tape, red pencils, discount charts, tip cards (these estimate approximate tips at 15% and 20%), bank slips, deposit slips, old checkbooks, and price lists. These inspirational tools should stimulate a math/logic student to enjoy some very creative time.
  - ✔ **Idea bucket:** Fill this bucket with craft items, including paper doilies, colored scented pens, foils, stars, glue, scissors, craft paper, pipe cleaners, and wallpaper books.
  - ✔ **Science bucket:** Fill this bucket with different types of magnifying glasses, retractable ruler, puzzles of dinosaurs, copies of science magazine, 3-D glasses and book, and a magnet and collection of items that may or may not be magnetic.
  - ✔ **Measuring bucket:** Fill this bucket with a large-sized tape measure and other measuring items such as a protractor and compass. Provide graph paper and a clipboard, as well as calligraphy pens.

✔ **Writing bucket:** Design this bucket for the creative writer in your class. Put a clipboard in the bucket and a variety of different pens, such as fine tips and those with a gripper on the shaft. Provide lined paper and alphabet strips in both manuscript and cursive. Put age-appropriate stationary in the bucket along with envelopes. Laminate a list of places to write to for free materials. Place the list in the box for students who want to write a letter requesting free materials and assure them that you will mail it for them. Make a mock letter as a guideline, laminate it, and place it in the bucket.

Instead of the bucket idea for middle school students, free time activities should involve technology, listening to additional material on tape with earphones, working at a computer on review material, joining in a small group discussion of class material, and library passes.

- *Involving parents:* Understanding brain-based teaching helps us see how critical it is that we consider the interests of the whole child for successful learning. If we want to truly change educational environments we will want to involve the child's total learning community.

One way to involve parents is to provide "Parent Packs," which are individual game packs designed to be sent home to parents of elementary students. The purpose of the packet is to provide a game that reinforces a skill being taught in school that can be practiced at home. The packs include games, game pieces, and directions.

As a teacher, I found grant writing to be an outstanding way to add new ideas, materials, and experiences to the classrooms I guided. One of my most successful grant projects involved the creation of Parent Packs. I knew I wanted to get parents involved with engaging educational experiences outside of my room. I felt they needed some incentive to play learning games with their children; so I created Parent Packs. The grant paid for my initial output for materials, but the basic idea is easily reproduced.

I created 10 different activity games parents could do with their children. The packs included typed directions and other ideas of how the games could be used. I contacted the local high school special education department and gave those students a project of stenciling 8½" x 11" envelopes with the words "Parent Packs" and had them label the contents on the outside. The special education students traced my patterns, colored them and then laminated the pieces for reproduction. I then began circulating the packets to my parents. I kept a record of who had what packet on a clipboard hanging by my classroom door and sent home a new packet each week. The packs were so popular other teachers began to request them for their parents. The special education department voted to subsidize the students and they began producing the packs as a money-making project. They also sold the packs at different school fairs throughout the district and used the money they made to take a class trip to an amusement park. This small grant idea inspired many families and students.

Improving Your Classroom Environment

Your classroom needs to convey a positive mood and message to the students in your care. Your room can convey a sense of purpose and security. Here are some guidelines for creating an atmosphere in your room that is designed for the age level you teach:

- *Kindergarten through Grade 3*

  During this early developmental stage, the classroom should offer remembrances of home, including comfort, warmth, and structure.

  ✔ Rugs and carpeted areas create centers that suggest separate rooms.

  ✔ Choose soothing colors and warm materials. Fabric on chairs in centers should be soft, inviting to the touch and restful in its coloration.

  ✔ The teacher will manage most of the equipment and will slowly introduce responsibility.

  ✔ Recess time is offered at least twice a day.

  ✔ The illumination of the room adds to the atmosphere. Remember, the older you are, the more light your eyes need. At this very young age, lighting should be low level and natural whenever possible.

  ✔ *Focus at this grade level:* comfort, reassurance, and security.

- *Grades 4 through 6*

  From fourth through sixth grade, the classroom should offer opportunities to be a part of a team.

  ✔ Provide interesting seating for groups.

  ✔ The seating arrangements should be flexible and easy to move.

  ✔ Begin to use a sociogram to help you place students with new friends; avoid allowing students to pick their partners until the end of sixth grade when their brains are mature enough to handle this better.

  ✔ Provide activities that use groups and clubs, teams, and partners to encourage working together.

  ✔ Structure is evident but opportunities to work independently are also available.

  ✔ Computers are important pieces of equipment at this age.

  ✔ Provide erase boards for student use.

✔ Assignment books are introduced and uniform places to return papers are available.

✔ Lighting level of illumination in room is average.

✔ *Focus at this grade level:* reaching out, collaboration.

- *Grades 6 through 8*

  From sixth grade to eighth grade the student most often only uses a room for one period; therefore, materials are often carried and not stored in the room. Lockers and schedules are introduced as the student begins to interact with more than one teacher.

  ✔ The room should be a control center that offers strong organizational features. Available schedules are posted and checked off when completed.

  ✔ Study skills are modeled and tape recorders, daily planners, and long-range planning calendars are all evident.

  ✔ The lighting level is normal to bright for daily use.

  ✔ *Focus at this grade level:* planning and organization

- *Grades 9 through 12*

  The room should offer unique seating arrangements that provide for independent student study and organization as well as very large group assembly.

  ✔ The feeling of the classroom is "office-like" and it is designed for efficiency and larger group instruction.

  ✔ State of the art technology is part of the instruction.

  ✔ Bulletin boards are often dedicated to learning new material or access to resources such as listing web pages and library computer hours.

  ✔ Brighter lighting is offered.

  ✔ *Focus at this grade level:* execute; Stand and deliver!

We underrate our brain and our intelligence . . .
Reluctance to learn cannot be attributed to the brain.
Learning is the brain's primary function, its constant
concern, and we become restless and frustrated if there
is no learning to be done. We are all capable of huge
and unsuspected accomplishments without effort.

—*Frank Smith*

Brain-Compatible Educational Activities

Learning is an active process for the brain, and you will want to provide multiple activities that support this interaction. The following pages contain activities that encourage small group interaction, understanding, self-concept, and shared responsibility. These activities will highlight the components of instruction that we have learned are critical in making experiences count. Four simple steps will guide you to accomplish the learning activities. Here are the four steps:

Focus   Goal or overview of the activity

Assemble   Materials needed and how to prepare them

Connect   Procedure for the activity

Transform   Adding dimension to the activity and understanding its value

Your Turn, My Turn

Focus

To encourage group conversation and turn-taking

Assemble

Fill a coffee can with colored tongue depressors or Popsicle® sticks. There should be five of each color. When students move into small groups for work activities or cooperative learning, place one can on the table in front of each group. Tell each student to remove five sticks of the same color and place them in front of himself.

Connect

Start the group activity. Every time a student talks or shares a comment, she places a stick in the can. When a student has no sticks remaining, she must refrain from talking.

Transform

This system helps the reluctant and/or quiet student join in the group more readily, and it helps the student who talks too much and tends to take over the group to self-monitor.

Note: This activity will only work well when a specific time frame for group work is designated. Use this for sessions that will not last longer than 15 to 20 minutes.

I Can Read You

Focus

To read various facial expressions

Assemble

Old magazines, yearbooks, catalogs, paper bags to hold pictures, glue, paper, and scissors. Cut pictures of faces showing various emotions from the printed materials. Place the faces in a paper bag.

Connect

Have students work in pairs. One person in each pair pulls one face out of the bag and asks the other person to act out the expression shown on the picture. The partners then name the emotion. Partners take turns pulling out faces and acting out the expressions for one another.

Transform

Have students cut out just the eyes, then just noses, then ears, etc. Paste the facial elements on paper to make a face collage, and complete the rest of face with crayons and pens. Have students label the expression conveyed by the collage face. Share the collages with the rest of the class.

Teamwork Creations[1]

Focus

To help a class group develop team unity and connectedness

Assemble

Large 11" x 17" paper folded accordion style in thirds, markers, paper clips (large)

Connect

Divide the class into groups of three. Give each group a topic to illustrate, such as one of the following:

- First spacecraft on Mars
- Homework-doing invention
- Undersea monster
- Animated superstar
- Olympic mascot.

Student #1 draws the top third of the illustration and folds his picture under so no one else can see it. Student #2 draws the middle and folds it under. Student #3 draws the bottom third of the illustration. Use the paper clip to hold down each section of the picture. After the last third of the picture has been completed, have the students remove the clips and label the picture.

Transform

Have students write stories about the characters or objects they created and share the results with the class.

[1]The idea for this activity was sparked by "Draw a Design," p. 65 in *NICE* by Kaplan, et al. (1977).

Whole Class Rocks[1]

Focus

To have the entire class set goals, monitor progress, and reach stated goals

Assemble

8½" x 11" tag board, bulletin board space, felt markers

Connect

Have the class set a goal for the entire group. (The goal can include a class trip, time to watch a video or movie, a special event with another class, etc.)

Write the class goal on the tag board. Advertise the reward by attaching it to the bulletin board.

Specify the observable behaviors your students must display in order to earn a check or tally and how many checks or tallies must be earned in order to reach the goal. For example, your class might earn a tally for problem-free recess, keeping the room in reasonable order, and no tattling or reporting on others for one hour. Have the class provide input into the types of behaviors they must exhibit.

Have one student a day record class results by placing tallies on the goal card when you report observing them. Select a different student to take on this responsibility daily or weekly.

When the required number of tallies is recorded, help the class plan and enjoy the event they have earned.

Transform

This activity provides immediate feedback for positive group behaviors, and allows students to work together as a team toward a common goal.

---

[1]The idea for this activity was sparked by "Monthly motivators class goals," p. 121 in *NICE* by Kaplan, et al. (1977).

All About You[1]

Focus

To turn the silhouette of each student's head or body into something special to take home and keep

Assemble

large brown craft paper or butcher paper, felt markers

Connect

Give each student an opportunity to be a special silhouette for a specified period of time.

Have students outline one another's profile or complete body outline on large pieces of craft or butcher paper.

Hang groups of these silhouettes on the bulletin board for a week.

During a designated period of time (after lunch, before recess, before the morning bell rings, etc.), have other students draw and/or write something positive about the silhouetted person.

When the silhouette is complete, encourage the student to take it home to share with family members.

Transform

Extend this activity by having students make silhouettes of different learning styles. For example, make a silhouette of a head that contains pictures of things an auditory learner would enjoy, such as CDs, a radio, or someone talking. Make a head for each different multiple intelligence type. Fill the heads with things each type would enjoy.

[1]The idea for this activity was sparked by "Special silhouettes," p. 131 in *NICE* by Kaplan, et al. (1977).

Personal Goal Chart

Focus

To help students set personal goals throughout the week

Assemble

three colored 3" x 5" cards (pink, yellow, green), white 3" x 5" index cards, envelope

On a green card, print the words, "I reached my goal."

On a yellow card, print "I came close to accomplishing my goal, but need to continue working on it."

On a blue card, print "I did not accomplish my goal and need to try harder next week."

Write the words "Individual Goals" on a bulletin board or experience chart.

Connect

Explain to students that they can plan to improve behavior, study habits, responsibility, etc., on a weekly basis. Have each student select one area in which she wants to improve. For example, a student might want to return homework regularly. Have the student write the goal on a white 3" x 5" card on Monday and place it in an envelope. On Friday have the student look at the card in the envelope and make a judgement as to whether she accomplished the goal. Have her place a colored index card that corresponds to the level that she met the goal on the bulletin board. Have one class member total the number of each color of cards and write the results on the board. The student might write, "70% of students in our class accomplished their personal goals, 20% came very close, and 10% will work on their same goals again next week."

Transform

This is an activity that students can also do in learning centers and in small group work. You can also assign numbers rather than colors for the format.

My Voice Counts[1]

Focus

To voice an opinion in a game of personal opinion statements. To think for one's self.

Assemble

Write personal opinion statements on 3" x 5" cards. Students can help you with this task. Write statements such as "Everyone watches too much TV," "Students should be allowed to determine what time they go to bed at night," "Students should receive a salary to go to school," "Money can buy happiness," and "Students should vote at 15 years of age."

Make a game board from a sheet of 24" by 24" tag paper. The board contains a ladder with 20 steps. Every third step has a rung marked "Shout Out." At top of ladder, is cartoon person who appears to be shouting with hands raised positively.

You will need a game spinner with the numbers 1, 2, and 3 and a game token for each player.

Connect

The starting player spins the spinner and moves that number of spaces up ladder. If the player lands on a rung marked "Shout out," he or she draws a statement card and voices an opinion on the subject. Other players may also voice their personal opinions about the card drawn and give reasons for whether they agree or disagree with the first opinion. Players rotate turns until the game ends.

Transform

Try this same activity with students learning another language.

---

[1]The idea for this activity was sparked by "Stand up and shout," p. 155 in *NICE* by Kaplan, et al.

Class Vote

Focus

This activity is a way to poll opinions in class on a regular basis. This allows students to focus on different issues and feel as if they have a right to voice their own opinions.

Assemble

Make a large "Thumbs Up, Thumbs Down" poster that shows a thumb pointing up and one pointing down next to it. Hang the poster at front of the room. Make smaller thumbs for desktops or notebooks.

Connect

Let students know their opinions count. As opportunities arise throughout the day, ask them to vote in instances such as the following:

- "Show me 'thumbs up' if you want recess now, 'thumbs down' if you want it after lunch."

- "Show me 'thumbs up' if you will want to have extra time on the written test or 'thumbs down' if you do not need the time."

- "Show me 'thumbs up' if you prefer to print the assignment and 'thumbs down' if you want to write in cursive."

Point to the poster as you ask students to express their opinions. Students will get used to being asked to form opinions on numerous types of activities within the classroom and feel more connected with the classroom community.

Transform

Start a web site for the class where students can record their polls and opinions and share them with other students. Use a program to create spreadsheets and graphs to show class results. Post the results weekly.

New Millenium Communication

Focus

To help students connect with a class message board, web page, or news group and to access it from computers in the building or at home (for students with access to the Internet)

Assemble

Set up a class Internet presence, such as a web page or news group. Make a list of students' web and Internet addresses (with parents' written permission) and give a copy to each student.

Software and information on how to set up your own class web page is available at **www.edumatch.com/dctb**.

Connect

Let students post messages for friends in other classes on the class web page. Post homework assignments, special announcements, new addresses, etc., on a weekly basis on the web page and encourage students to check the page often.

Transform

Let a different student be the editor of the class web page each week. The student is responsible for updating the page, making corrections, and making sure all information is correct.

Brainstorming Activities

Focus

To brainstorm and create ideas for writing assignments. These activities begin to train the brain to look for details and meaning before you write.

Assemble

interesting pictures of events, writing materials

Connect

Use the three O's for brainstorming.

1. *Observe details*
   Have students look at a picture and find five things in it that they can identify and name. Have them list the five things. Then have them write five words about each one of the five things they saw. Ask students to use the items they have written as the basis for writing sentences about the picture.

2. *Observe description*
   Have students attend a performance (play, assembly, oral book report, etc.) When it is complete, ask students to write five things they remember about the activity. They should be concrete things and not opinions. With the five observations in front of them as a cue, ask students to write a paragraph about what they observed.

3. *Observe opinion*
   Have students write one thing they liked about the picture they observed (in number 1) and one thing they did not like. Or have them write one thing about what they watched in number 2. Have them choose one of the opinions and write a paragraph that supports the opinion.

Remember, in brainstorming you want to provide a background of experiences, generate new ideas, and aid in structuring content.

Transform

Have students use a computer outlining program, such as *Expressions*, to develop further interest in writing. See the Resource section for more information on this software.

Thinking Cap

Focus

To help students learn how to problem solve and to begin to develop logical thinking patterns. At least once a week during morning meeting time, designate five to ten minutes as "thinking cap" times. Tell students, "Put on your thinking caps and get ready to do some brain work."

Assemble

Collect a group of questions and place them on index cards. Color code the questions by category and level of difficulty. Here are some typical questions to include:

Basic Reasoning
- Do you feel happier when you are with people or by yourself?
- How many eggs can you hold in your hand at one time?
- You can eat with your hands. What else can you do with them?

Comprehension
- Would you like to go underwater and live in an undersea lab?
- How many eyelashes do you think you have?
- How do you know when a cat is happy?

Word Finding
- Name all the people you know whose name starts with S.
- Name all the sounds you hear at a farm.
- Name all the people who play games for a living.

Advanced thinking
- Two people ran out of a room quickly. What could cause them to do that?
- Why do people sleep in beds?
- What is the difference between a left-handed person and a right-handed person?

Connect

Have a student randomly draw one of the question cards and read it aloud. Then have a class discussion that centers around the question. Monitor student participation carefully to provide everyone with an opportunity to express his or her thoughts.

Transform

Hold up a large box. Ask the class, "What could we do with this box?" Encourage creative responses and offer suggestions such as, "Could I make it into a boat?" or "Could I sell it on ebay?"

IF You Were[1]

Focus

To help students make decisions and comparisons. This activity encourages the development of skills for comparison and contrast.

Assemble

Write a group of questions on index cards that begin with the phrase, "If you were." Here are some examples:

- If you were climbing a mountain, which would you rather use: a pick or a pair of hiking boots?
- If you were in a snowstorm, which would you rather have: heavy gloves or snowshoes?
- If you were caught in the rain, which would you rather have: an umbrella or a raincoat?

Connect

Keep the questions with you and use them anytime your class has down time, such as waiting for a bus for a field trip or when waiting in the gym or auditorium for an assembly to begin.

Pick a card at random and ask students to picture themselves in the situation. Encourage them to visualize the situation before providing an answer. When students do answer, have them provide reasons for their choices.

Transform

Cut pictures of various actions from magazines that show a problem being solved or a task being performed (a car in a service station being repaired, a woman making breakfast, Dad loading clothes into a washing machine). Show each picture to your students and ask four questions:

- What is happening?
- What should they do?
- What do you think will happen next?
- Did that take care of the job?

[1]From Jones (1994)

Events of the Day

Focus

To mark the passage of time using color. This is a helpful technique to help students plan quickly and learn self-direction.

Assemble

Selection of 3" x 5" or smaller colored pieces of construction paper (at least 10 different colors) and one 3" x 5" or smaller piece of aluminum foil

Connect

Place the pieces of paper near your front bulletin board or chalkboard. Assign one color to each activity in your daily schedule. Tape a colored piece of paper on the board next to each individual item on your schedule. Each time an activity is over ask a student to remove the colored square from your board. Place the piece of foil next to each activity on the schedule *as* it is being completed.

Transform

Make a paper chain with one link for each activity on the daily calendar. Have a student cut off the corresponding link from the bottom up as the day progresses.

Theme Days

Focus

To add variety and interest to a typical class day by providing a daily theme. The brain responds to "linking" activities and then encodes these series of learning experiences.

Assemble

Select a theme for the day. Here are some suggestions:
- rainbow day
- salute to an author day
- recognize a hero day
- honor a famous artist day
- tribute to a country or place day

Gather information, clippings, artifacts, symbols, pictures, and visuals that feature your selected topic. Offer activities all day based on your theme.

Connect

For this example, Rainbow Day is the theme. Here are some ways to reinforce the theme:
- Hang strips of crepe paper in the doorway in rainbow-ordered colors so students can walk through a rainbow to enter the classroom.
- Play the song "Somewhere Over the Rainbow" as students enter.
- Borrow prisms from the science lab and place them throughout the room.
- Have students use colored pens to complete daily work. Offer rainbow-hued lead mechanical pencils.
- Make a rainbow paper chain and place it at the front of the class. Write a fact or question about rainbows and/or color on each link. Have a student come forward once every hour, take off a link, and read it (Examples: What is the exact order of the colors in a rainbow? Where are we most likely to see rainbows? What causes a rainbow to occur?).

Transform

Have students design pretend "Tattoos" on a rainbow theme.

Penny Jar

Focus

To stimulate creative thinking through an enrichment activity

Assemble

large plastic clear jar with cover, multiple items of the same object (pennies, paper clips, marbles), small slips of paper, envelope

Connect

Each week fill the jar with a different selection of items. Have students try to guess the exact amount of items in the jar. Place the slips of paper and an envelope near the jar. Students write their guesses and names on the slips of paper and put them in the envelope. (You might limit each student to a certain amount of guesses per week.) Count the items in the jar at the end of the week, compare the guesses, and declare the person who made the closest guess the winner. Award the winner a prize, such as a homework coupon, pencil, free time coupon, etc.

Transform

Change the item container to one that is tall and narrow or wide and flat. Discuss estimation, size, prediction, etc., with your students as they submit their choices.

> Read the best books first, or you may not have a chance to read them all.
>
> —*Thoreau*

Brain-Based Strategies for Reading, Math, and Writing

Reading

Researchers are now able to help us learn more about how students read, as well as how effective intervention strategies can be. Using the PET scan and other neuroimaging machines we have learned that students learn to read in what researcher Ken Pugh at Yale University refers to as a three-part process (2001):

1. seeing the visual symbol and recognizing the letter
2. performing the phonological process of associating sound to symbol
3. deriving word meaning via semantic processes.

A skilled reader will incorporate all three steps at a very rapid rate. The process is literally automatic. If a step of this process is missing, the reader will struggle. Pugh's work has been unable to see the success of pure sight word reading, which would avoid step two. He believes that interventions that rely on phonics are far more effective that those that rely on sight interpretation.

Phonemic Awareness

What is phonemic awareness? This term refers to an understanding of how spoken language is linked to written language. Specifically, it is the ability to first *distinguish* and then *manipulate* the individual sound units, or phonemes, in words. (Abbott et al., 2002). There are 44 English phoneme sounds and 26 letters in the alphabet. Current research suggests that phonemic awareness is a strong predictor of later reading achievement.

> "Current research suggests that phonemic awareness is a strong predictor of later reading achievement."

The following page lists four phonics programs that are highly recommended based on their validities and success rates with developing readers.

Four Outstanding Phonics Programs Using Brain-Based Principles

1. *Orton Gillingham-Based Multisensory Structured Language Approach:* This technique in particular uses VAKT (visual/auditory/kinesthetic/tactile) teaching. It uses all learning pathways in the brain simultaneously in order to enhance memory and learning.

2. *Lindamood Bell Learning Process:* This program develops three sensory cognitive processes that underlie basic language processing. The three processes are language comprehension and thinking, word attack and spelling, and visual motor functions. It helps students be aware of how sounds feel as they say them. It adds visualization and memory techniques.

3. *Alphabetic Phonics:* This is a guided discovery approach for teaching new concepts that actively engages students and helps develop higher level thinking skills. It introduces the alphabet with sound relationships.

4. *The Spalding Method:* This is a total language arts approach consisting of integrated, simultaneous, multisensory instruction in listening and reading comprehension, speaking, writing, spelling, and phonics. It is more structured than the other techniques and doesn't always adapt to the style of the non-conventional learner. It works best with concrete, sequential students.

One helpful software program created to increase auditory processing and phonemic awareness is *Earobics®*. This program helps students develop phonological awareness and phonics skills through a variety of auditory and visual techniques and drills. Dr. Paula Tallal and Dr. Michael Merzenich have developed a computer-based phonics program for language-impaired students called *Fast Forward®*. It slows down phoneme processes and enables the student to discriminate between sounds. After initial instruction on the computer, the student can actually guide himself or herself through further programs as the complexity increases. (See the Resource section in the back of this book for further information on *Earobics®* and *Fast Forward®*.)

Reading and Brain Research

Early research using neuroimaging indicates that excellent readers have developed strong left hemisphere brain activity and literally rely on the language center of the brain when reading. Poor readers seem to shift reading responsibility to the right hemisphere and other areas of the brain, which are not as receptive. Thus, the poor reader loses valuable connections and encoding possibilities. To increase reading mastery, Pugh suggests we teach activities to strengthen the left hemisphere of the brain that leads to reading mastery.

Teacher Tip: Readers who use the left hemisphere (language-based strengths) are more successful readers.

Patricia Wolfe investigated PET scans of a reader and reported the results in her book *Brain Matters*. These scans showed significant frontal lobe activity occurs when a student read silently, *more so* than when he or she is reading aloud to others. Activity in the frontal lobes often indicates higher-level thinking. On the other hand, the scan of the student reading aloud showed activity in the motor area of the brain that governs speech while showing little activity elsewhere (Wolfe, 2001). This research helps us see why it is important to balance silent and oral reading experiences to acquire diagnostic information on decoding problems and how to enhance comprehension of what is being read. Just one technique alone eliminates the opportunity for further growth.

Teacher Tip: Readers must use both oral and silent reading experiences to stimulate frontal lobes, thus resulting in higher-level thinking. Use oral reading to build speech and silent reading to build comprehension and recall.

You can envision reading as a multi-step process. Each developing step requires the preceding step to make it happen. The main "floor" preceding the staircase is phonetic awareness and the ability to process the sound elements of language. Each step following takes the process to a more sophisticated layer of the brain. The eventual culminating step leads to a process that is now automatic and totally absorbed by the brain. The brain is now immersed in a total language experience with reading.

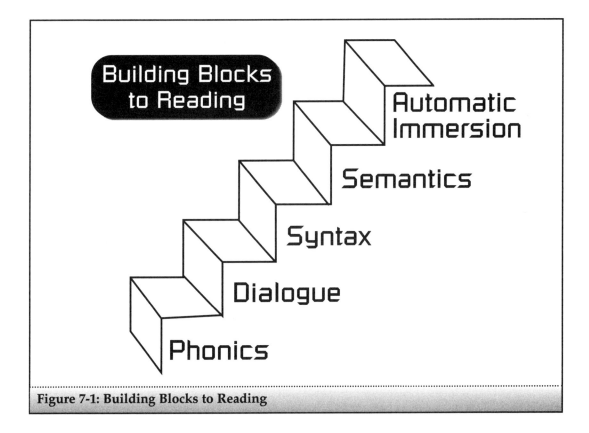

Figure 7-1: Building Blocks to Reading

Math

> Do not concern yourself with your difficulties in mathematics.
> I assure you that mine are still greater.
>
> — *Albert Einstein, in a letter to a student*

The **parietal**, or top part of the brain is the home to calculation and orientation with the left side specifically active in the production of mathematics. It is during the first four years of life that the brain develops an innate sense for math and for logic. Very rapid absorption of patterns, design, logic, and estimation are evident up to age four. Learning style inclinations for math are predominantly tactile followed by visual. Auditory is not a strong preference for learning math.

Math instruction requires multisensory techniques, including the use of hands-on manipulatives for students. Any object can serve as a manipulative. Begin to collect items such as rice, rocks, macaroni, beans, paper punch dots, and dice to use as math manipulatives in your classroom.

Color can enhance recall of math processes and steps. It can be used to teach the different symbols and signs. For example, introduce a color scheme to aid in recall and transfer of math symbols. Try red for addition, green for subtraction, blue for multiplication, and purple for division. Provide students with highlighters so they can mark the signs on their papers themselves.

Support different learning styles in math by offering a variety of materials that students can use to help them as they begin to discover the transfer in math from object to symbol.

Left to Right Progression
As you introduce basic math addition activities, show number relationship by placing a token or object next to each numeral the child is learning.

Initially, introduce placing the object immediately beside the numeral, in a normal left to right progression. This is the direction the eyes will follow first; therefore, introduce this format before column addition. Here's an example of a left-to-right progression. The dots represent the objects:

4 •••• + 5 ••••• =

When students are comfortable with horizontal number sentences, introduce the vertical pattern

4 ••••

+5 •••••

Finally, introduce the total cluster as a pattern:

$$4$$
$$\underline{+\,5}$$

• • • • • • • •

Count on

Use the language term "count on" to help students recognize that they are adding on to an existing groups of numbers so they do not have to go back and count each number again. For example, in the problem above you would say, "Four, count on five," rather than "1, 2, 3, 4, plus 1, 2, 3, 4, 5." Start with the smaller number and using your fingers to show it as a fist, say, "Count on 4." Make a fist for 4 and have the child count onto it, saying, "5, 6, 7, 8, 9."

Column Addition

When instructing column addition, show students how to cluster groups of like numbers together rather than just counting each number. Here are two examples:

7

2

1     $1 + 1 = 2$, $7 + 2 = 9$, $5 + 4 = 9$; therefore, $9 + 9$ are $18 + 2 = 20$

5

1

4

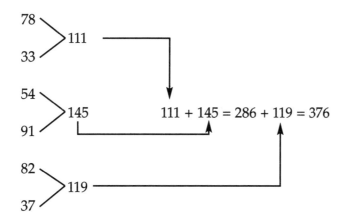

$111 + 145 = 286 + 119 = 376$

Paper Helpers

- *Graph paper:* Students often have difficulty learning the concept of regrouping or borrowing when they are learning subtraction. If you find that to be the case with your students, have them figure their problems on one-inch graph paper. This helps students "see" numbers in columns and it helps keep them from confusing the information.

- *Notebook paper:* Another way to introduce a column to a double-digit math problem is to take a regular piece of loose leaf notebook paper and place it horizontally. The student now sees columns from top to bottom and writes numerals in this format. As the student becomes successful using the paper and moves into three and four column problems, take a dark marker and put in a vertical line after every third column (before the thousand, million, and billion columns).

- *Computer paper:* Use computer paper with its alternating green and white lines to teach students initially how to work a problem from left to right. Then use it later when they are subtracting two- and three-column work. Place the top number on green and the lower number on white with the answer on green. This gives meaning to the processes that must occur in the lower numbers. You can easily punch this paper to fit into a standard-sized notebook.

Multiplication

If we apply the notion of brain-based theory in learning the multiplication facts, we would take what the brain knows first and build from that as the association. By the time students are introduced to the process of multiplication, most students can count by twos and by fives. Therefore, when we introduce multiplication we should start by teaching the twos and fives first. Our assumption for this is because the chances are that the child has totally assimilated the pattern of twos and fives in his long-term memory and we can build new information on that knowledge base. This established base of facts should make recall faster. Once you can see that students are in control of these two facts, introduce the ones and zeros, and then tens and elevens. These facts are immediately visual and have a rhythmic pattern. Now the student should know the zeros, ones, twos, fives, tens and elevens. Next, introduce the number nine, as this unique number has a novel format that will attract the brain's interest for variety. Teach your students to use these tricks for learning their nines:

Magic 9 — the answers when multiplying nine all add up to nine

- $1 \times 9 = 9$
- $2 \times 9 = 18$ $(1 + 8 = 9)$
- $3 \times 9 = 27$ $(2 + 7 = 9)$
- $4 \times 9 = 36$ $(3 + 6 = 9)$
- $5 \times 9 = 45$ $(4 + 5 = 9)$
- $6 \times 9 = 54$ $(5 + 4 = 9)$

- $7 \times 9 = 63$ $(6 + 3 = 9)$
- $8 \times 9 = 72$ $(7 + 2 = 9)$
- $9 \times 9 = 81$ $(8 + 1 = 9)$
- $9 \times 10 = 90$ $(9 + 0 = 9)$

Learning to Multiply by Nine on Your Fingers:

This is a whole to part, visual-tactile approach. It is especially successful with students who demonstrate right-brained priority.

- Hold your ten fingers out in front of you, palms down. Count whatever number you wish to multiply 9 by, from left to right, on your fingers. Put that finger down. The number of fingers on the left side of the lowered finger is the tens of the answer; the number of fingers on the right side represents the ones. For example, pretend you wanted the answer to 5×9. Count on your fingers to five, starting with your left little finger. Five is your left thumb, so turn it down. There are four fingers to the left and five fingers to the right of the turned thumb, therefore $9 \times 5 = 45$ (Mastropieri, 1991, p. 87).

This leaves the sixes, sevens and eights to be learned. Introduce them in snappy verbal patterns or with mnemonics. For example, say, "Six times three now don't be mean, six times three is just eighteen." There are several commercially-available math tapes to help students learn the remainder of their facts by pattern and music. See the Resource section for *Math Facts on Tape*.

Touch Math is a commercially-available math program that introduces physical movement (touching specific places on each numeral to increase recall) to learning numbers. It is very helpful for left-brained preference learners and those who are kinesthetic/tactile.

Visual Math Cues

Students with visual memory recall often confuse different math processes and are not sure where to begin when they start a problem. They need cues to start working and should learn strategies that help them continue solving a problem and ultimately solve it. One way to encourage continuity is to use "red light, green light" to encourage where to stop and start. Highlight columns when borrowing or regrouping with green so students know where to look first. Then place a small red dot over numbers they have used.

893 (Shaded area would be green.)   952
-34   x42 (Dot would appear in red.)
                                         1004

Long Division

Long division can be difficult for some students because it requires multiple steps that must be done in the correct order. Students who struggle with this are unable to recall each step and end up leaving one out. Try a mnemonic to help students remember each step.

In long division there are five separate steps required to solve a problem:

D ivide

M ultiply

S ubtract

C ompare

B ring Down

Here are some mnemonic sentences to help your students remember the key steps in long division. Have your class create their own special mnemonics when you introduce the different steps and encourage individual students to create their own.

- **David Makes Silly Cartoon Bats.**
- **Does McDonalds Sell CheeseBurgers Downtown?**
- "Have your family help you do long division: **Dad, Mother, Sister, Cousin,** and **Brother.** Then your **Dad** comes back to check it all again."

All Ears On Board!

Some students will need to talk quietly to themselves when they work math problems. This auditory/motor activity aids the focus on the different math steps and acts as a personal cue. This way a student "hears" his voice as he visualizes the steps. At times, however, this technique can be bothersome to fellow classmates if it is too loud. Model whispering and verbal mediation for students or provide a separate place, like a cloakroom or behind a screen, for this type of study.

Word Problems

Help students who struggle with story problems to learn a variety of techniques when they work on these types of problems. Tell them they need to act like detectives when they work on story problems. Explain to them that just like a detective, they need to figure out the clues in a story problem. Teach your students the steps on the next page in order to become story problem detectives.

A Detective Solves the Problem!

1. The detective highlights the number clues and reads the problem out loud.

2. The detective uses a different color highlighter to highlight the words that tell the detective what to do.

3. The detective visualizes the problem by drawing a picture illustrating what is happening in the situation.

4. The detective asks questions, such as "If then, what?"

   - *If the items are being combined,* ***then*** *the answer should be bigger.* (Tanner and Jennifer each have six blocks. How many do they have altogether?)

   - *If the items are being shared,* ***then*** *the answer should be smaller.* (Jackson had nine videos. He gave two to his sister Lindsay. How many does he have now?)

5. The detective solves the problem! The detective then rechecks the computation to see if the answer makes sense.

The use of a highlighter helps the student break down the problem into simple steps. Students can use yet another color to highlight the key **number language words in the problem**. Number language words are words and phrases that refer to or explain quantity or amount. Make a cue card of key number language words such as *how many, greater than, less than, how many in all, how many all together, how many remaining,* etc. Post the cue card on a bulletin board or place it where all students can see it while they attempt story problems. You might make a small copy for each student to keep at his or her desk.

Writing

> Effective writing requires the application of
> multiple memory functions in the brain.
>
> — *Dr. Mel Levine (1994, p. 187)*

Writing involves a complex pattern of output through the brain that requires several different pathways to occur. To write, the brain must assemble and orchestrate multiple skills and functions. The process of writing requires three steps:

1. Language Production (formulating the ideas to write)
2. Fine Motor Function (following through with the physical production of writing)
3. Visual Motor Memory (the ability to see, hold on to the language, and actually write it)

Here's a more concrete example of how writing occurs:

1. The brain formulates in sequential memory what it wants to write and sends a message to the hand.
2. The brain then directs specific muscles and nerves to hold the pencil while it directs other muscles/nerves to move it to form the letter symbols.
3. Tiny nerve endings in the fingers report back to the brain on what they are doing and the activity of writing occurs.

To help students develop writing skills we must introduce writing as a series of steps. Only when each step is completed do we have a finished project. Writing activities must encourage the brain to do the following:

1. **Create** a thought.
2. **Develop** the order of the thought.
3. **Follow Through** with the motor activity.

The Tools

Writing is a very physical process for the learner. We need both body and brain to work together to produce the written product. Writing is a total effort that involves integrated action. It does not just involve the fingers alone! All steps are related and connected in writing.

As an educator, build a foundation for writing by offering basic implements. The list on the next page describes some basic writing tools.

Writing Tools

- A wooden or plastic clipboard gives the writer a firm surface that can be carried anywhere.

- Offer different mediums for the writer's hands. Try large markers, pencils with built-in grippers, and pencil pillows. Mechanical pencils are more fluid than regular lead pencils and can be purchased with built-in grippers of multiple types.

- When purchasing rubber grippers for pencils, stay away from flat triangular ones and instead buy the chunky, "formed to the finger" grippers that occupational therapists assure us are more suitable for the physical pincer grip required for writing.

- Use large sheets of paper for brainstorming activities and group writing projects.

- Provide colorful markers for these brainstorming sessions.

- Use pastel-colored notebook paper at times to inspire change and interest in an activity that might otherwise feel tedious to some students.

- Begin teaching computer keyboard skills by third grade. Start with introducing a memory technique for learning the pattern of the letters on the keyboard, move to drill and practice, and incorporate interest and uniqueness in recall. Choose software that offers engaging activities while rehearsing the letter patterns. Some recommended titles are *Type to Learn* (Scholastic) and *Jump-Start Typing* (Knowledge Adventure).

- The use of non-carbonless notebook paper can help slower writers who have difficulty keeping up with notes. Have a student who takes exemplary notes write on the non-carbonless notepaper and, at the conclusion of class, give the copy to the student who needs to further add to his or her notes. (Caution: This is by no means a substitution for note-taking but rather an additional tool for support.) This technique is best used as an accommodation for a student with documented writing challenges.

Note-Taking as a Critical Part of Writing

Employ **active note-taking strategies** when you teach students how to organize and produce their notes. Most note-taking occurs during a lecture format, which is primarily a listening activity. Research indicates that the average retention rate after 24 hours for a lecture is less than 10 percent. Therefore, it is critical to keep the student's brain interested and focused during rote copying. Active note-taking will help a student keep "processing" while he or she writes notes and will add a more positive multisensory effect to the task. One way to encourage active thinking is to introduce the strategy of using the margin column as a cue to the brain during note-taking.

Point out the margin to your students and tell them that it is also called a **topic column**, which is used throughout the note-taking process. Demonstrate how this column is an area where they can jot down key words, thoughts, and write shorthand-type cues regarding the information they are writing. Show students how the margin column should become the critical activity part of their note-taking. Here are some ways students can use the margin:

- Write words they do not understand from the lecture and need to have clarified

- They can place a star in the margin, cueing themselves about information that must be learned for a test or place a question mark to cue themselves that they did not understand what they wrote.

- Instruct your students to never read over their notes without a colored pen in hand to circle key words, phrases, etc., and to make the margin column work for them.

- Remind your students that notes are best remembered when read over within eight hours of being recorded. This will link the information to longer recall for material and take advantage of the immediate learning experiences.

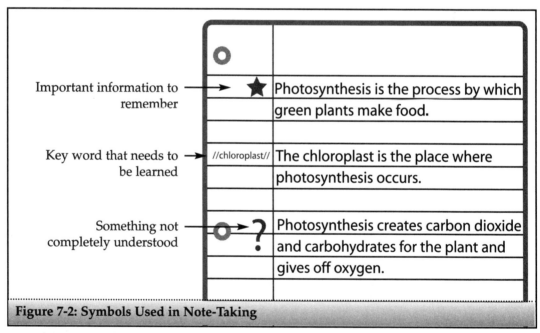

Figure 7-2: Symbols Used in Note-Taking

Often students who struggle with note-taking have poor short-term memory patterns and are unable to retain the material in their minds when they write. Therefore, they benefit from the visualization technique of **webbing** or **mapping** (called semantic webbing). A graphic organizer will help these students sort out the main ideas, highlight key supporting statements, and get a big picture of what they are writing. The use of semantic webbing is a prewriting strategy that can activate the brain's prior knowledge, clarify relationships among the ideas, and organize the idea into a meaningful written product. Research suggests that the process of putting material into a different format can enhance understanding and recall. Below are two typical examples of graphic organizer forms. Also look in the Resources section of this book for information on *Frameworks*, which are commercially made semantic maps. You can also print out pre-made visual organizers using the software program *Inspiration*.

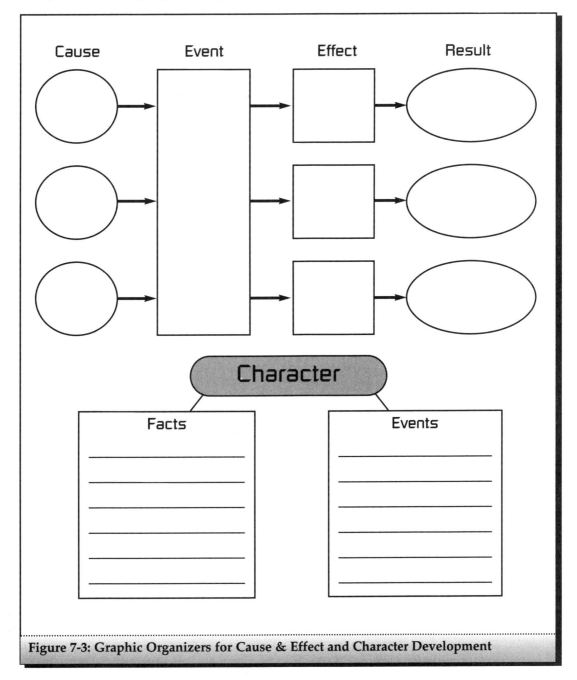

Figure 7-3: Graphic Organizers for Cause & Effect and Character Development

Encourage Active Listening
Use graphic organizers as a way to introduce new material or plan the school day (see Figure 6-1 on page 77). This visual tool shows students how the daily plan will look, and they can follow along with the order of your instruction. Pause frequently as you share new information and let students ask questions. Also, ask them questions to help them maintain their focus on the topic. Clarify the topic and encourage active participation by frequent follow-up and recall as you instruct.

Helping Students Take More Active Notes

- Provide a clipboard for note-taking.

- Allow your students to use a variety of writing instruments.

- Teach a webbing or mapping technique to help maintain interest in main ideas and the details of the lecture

- Encourage students to use the margin column as a cue for recall and learning

- Require students to use a highlighter when reviewing notes and have them circle and mark key information as they read.

- Suggest students read notes over again within eight hours of taking them and discuss them within two hours.

- Encourage auditory learners to read notes aloud into a tape recorder and play them back as they read notes again.

Figure 7-3: Encouraging Active Note-Taking

Feeding Your Brain

From academics to memory, activities to strategies, as educators we are trained in understanding the basic tools of learning, but what is less understood is what other areas may effect the children we are teaching every day. We know mental exercise is important to the brain and we have seen the results of how it can engage and challenge the mind. But what do we know about the impact of physical exercise on learning? As "environmental engineers," we need to understand that there are many areas within the environment that also effect learning. You can have the most exciting multisensory lesson plan ever designed ready for your class, but if your students are stressed, tired, or physically unfit, their learning ability and interest will be markedly decreased.

Physical Activity

We are all aware of the result and benefits of physical exercise. We see athletes on TV everyday who demonstrate increased muscle tone; firm, shapely bodies; and improved stamina and endurance. We know exercise helps the body, but what can it do for the brain? The results of a trio of studies presented at the 2001 Society for Neuroscience Conference suggests that regular exercise can improve cognitive function and increase levels of substances in the brain responsible for maintaining the health of neurons. This research indicated that regular physical exercise enhances memory function (Cocke, 2002). The principle researcher Dr. Carl Cotman, a neuroscientist at the University of California, states, "Exercise stimulates the production of all kinds of wonderful molecules that keep neurons strong. I think of them as molecular fertilizer. And exercise actually increases these molecules in the brain." These findings seem to suggest that you can change your brain chemistry with exercise!

When setting up your daily plan, allow time for exercise breaks and physical activity. Try not to eliminate recess or gym for a child as a punishment for unfinished classwork. In terms of human application to students in the classroom, offering a regular activity period such as gym or recess in addition to brief periods of in-room, stimulating movement should benefit the student. In addition to a well-run physical activity program offered by the physical education department, in-class physical activities such as those offered in *Brain Gym, Play Fair,* and *Energize* can add to students' rigor and stamina. Recent studies in the area of linking childhood behavior and mental ability found that more actively-engaged children create a more enriched environment for themselves than those offered by traditional educational enrichment programs. The most adventurous and curious learners had the highest IQ levels (Hotz, 2002).

Here are some ways to bring physical activity into your classroom:

1. **Hula Hoops**
    These plastic hoops, which were the rage in the 1960s, are still around and can provide a multitude of activities for quick breaks and restricted physical activities within the classroom. The hoop can be twirled, balanced, and tossed but also can create a structured space in which physical activities actually take place. Place a hoop on the floor for each student, and encourage the student to stand inside its boundaries. Lead the students through a variety of bending and stretching exercises while they stay within their individual hoops. This gives everyone his or her own individual place. You can also use the hoops in movement activities. Have students use their hoops to follow your step-by-step directions. You might say, "Stand in the center of your hoop. Bend over and pick up your hoop with both hands. Now move the hoop to your hips, your shoulders, your ankles, etc."

2. **Overhead Exercises**
    Use a marker to divide a plastic overhead sheet into eight blocks. Draw a stick figure doing a different stretching exercise in each block. Picture simple exercises such as touching toes, stretching arms above head, etc., and display the pictures on the overhead. Write the numbers 1-8 on small slips of paper and place them in a cup. Appoint someone from the class as the exercise leader for the day. Have this person come up front, draw a number from the cup, and point to that exercise on the overhead. Classmates then do five repetitions of the displayed exercise. Continue this brief motor break for approximately five minutes.

3. **Arm Bends**
    Have students select two books of similar size and shape. Instruct them to hold one book in each hand and lift their arms straight out from their body. Have them raise the books over their heads and then as far to each side as they can. Count to ten with the students as they all lift together. Encourage students to create their own ways to lift books and stretch their arms from their chairs and at their desks. Provide large elastic bands for further arm stretching at desk.

4. Deep Breathing, Visualization, and Meditation

Dr. Andrew Weil, nationally known physician and proponent of integrative medicine, is an advocate of deep breathing techniques. He maintains it is an important health strategy for anyone and that it can relieve stress, increase oxygen to the brain, and should be part of any health regime. Encourage your students to start each day with several deep breaths as they stand next to their desks ready to start the day.

Here are two exercises to help your students learn to relax their breathing:

1. Teach students to inhale slowly to a count of four. Tell them to imagine the warm air moving to all parts of the body. Pause, and then slowly exhale again counting to four. Ask students to imagine the tension floating out and away from their bodies. Pause, and then start the counting again for the inhale. Repeat this several times with students.

2. Tell children to try this activity at home. Have them lie on the floor in a quiet place and set a small book on their stomach. Then they should take a deep breath and slowly exhale. If the book slides off, the breath was deep enough; if not, they need to breath more deeply.

Remind students of their deep breathing techniques prior to tests and other stress-inducing activities such as oral book reports, presentations, etc.

Visualization

Here is an activity to teach visualization as a relaxation technique:

1. Have students sit in a comfortable position at their desks, on the floor, or sitting on their chairs in a straddle position, as if on horseback.

2. Ask students to discuss where they like to relax and what they are doing when they are most comfortable. Put several of their answers inside a circle drawn on the board.

3. Tell students to close their eyes and imagine their favorite spot where they feel most comfortable and relaxed. Tell them to visualize being in that place and its surroundings.

4. Tell students that as they imagine their place, you will slowly count to 60 while they keep their eyes closed and continually imagine their special place. Tell them that when you reach 60, they will take a deep breath and open their eyes.

Illustrate times when students might want to do this technique on their own, such as before a test, after a long day, on a noisy bus ride, etc.

Meditation

Meditation can also be modeled as a way of encouraging the brain to rest and slow down. You can have students choose a special word to say to themselves and concentrate on while listening to quiet classical music. Provide a brief minute each day for students to pause and contemplate their personal thoughts or simply sit quietly. This quiet time adds to focused awareness and perception.

The body has a physical reaction to the relaxed state you are trying to introduce by deep breathing, meditation, and visualization. Body metabolism will slow down, and nervous system activity will reduce its movement. The brain's electrical signals seem to work more in harmony and in a more regular synchronization as a result of these down times.

5. **Stretch Breaks**

Plan regular stretch breaks and have student helpers participate, plan, and implement them. Choose an appropriate musical selection to play during this break. Use the same choice each time. This will serve as a memory device and cue for your students. When the specific selection starts, students should immediately recognize the music and get ready for the stretch break. You might choose a marching song, a piece of lively Irish dance music, or a popular hit song.

Here are two enthusiastic chants and rhymes to use to encourage or introduce a stretch:

Shoulder, Waist, Toe!   *Ear, back, knee,*
Shoulder, Waist, Toe!   *Look at me!*
We are on the go!   *Head, back, shoe,*
Shoulder Waist Toe!   *Look at You!*

6. **Board Games**

Provide board games and small puzzles, pick-up sticks, crossword puzzles, chess boards, and unique marble and plastic challenge games as opportunities for free time. These thinking games offer a mental refresher and help students stay more engaged during free time.

7. **Plastic Golf Bag Tubes**

These tubes are available at a nominal fee at sports supply centers (garage sales are another great place to find these). Provide one tube for each student. Have each student hold the tube with hands spread apart and follow these directions: "Touch the front of your body with the tube. Now touch the top of your head. Touch your side. Bend forward to the front. Bend to the side. Bend to the other side. Bend slowly backwards." Have the students put their tubes on floor and follow these directions: "Stand behind the tube. Stand in front of the tube. Stand on the left side of the tube. Now stand on the right side."

8. **Yoga**

Recently, on a national level, several school districts have restricted formal physical education due to a lack of funds. Several teachers have recognized this deficit and have introduced yoga to their students. They practice yoga in class during a brief break in the morning and then again at the end of the day. Research has indicated that Tai Chi and Yoga can have a calming effect on the nervous system, and your students may benefit from this interaction in their busy lives.

9. **Phonics/ Exercise**

You can incorporate a learning activity while your students exercise. Have students combine the learning of phonics with body gestures and exercise by asking students to stand and repeat this verse (using a variety of letters and sounds):

Hands by lips say a letter (S)
Hands on hips say the sound (/s/)
Hands on ground
Say a word that starts with that sound. (snake)

Play the song "YMCA" by the Village People to lead your students in another spirited exercise song. Have students use their bodies to spell out the letters Y-M-C-A as they sing them during the chorus of the song.

Stress

Scientists are finding that the brain releases the hormone **cortisol** in stressful situations. Cortisol is a hormone that affects metabolism, the immune system, and the brain. Excessively high levels of cortisol alter the brain by making it vulnerable to processes that destroy brain cells, thereby producing a degeneration of brain tissue. It can reduce the number of connections in certain parts of the brain. We would like to avoid situations in our lives that might release this damaging chemical. From a positive sense, we have learned that children who have experienced a secure attachment to a parent are more adaptive and produce less cortisol.

Just as exercise can increase levels of the protein BDNF that nourishes and maintains neurons, stress has been shown to decrease BDNF levels in the same brain areas. (Cocke, 2002). Therefore, stress and anxiety can undermine the body's natural defenses, leaving people more vulnerable to flu, colds, and other maladies (Doughton, 2002). New research is revealing intricate links between the brain, that controls the body's response to stress, and the immune system, that fights disease.

You can't eliminate the stress in your students' lives, but you can teach them ways to cope with it daily. Your classroom can offer an environment that is safe, nurturing, and reassuring. As a professional you can respond with positive modeling behavior that eliminates tension and promotes learning. There are a variety of social modeling materials that can be used in the classroom and offer simple steps to positive management of stress. These are listed in the Resource section.

Seven Stress Busters

1. Play quiet music during the beginning of class and during transitions. Try music as a soft background calming technique. New Age music often helps relieve tension because of its lack of associations and demands on the listener. To learn how music has helped in treating neurological diseases and injuries go to http://www.musichaspower.org. (Tomaino, 2002). You might try selections from Kenny G, Yanni, Windham Hill (music label), or classical music such as the first movement of Beethoven's 6th (Pastorale) symphony or Pachelbel's Canon in D major.

2. Provide students with the opportunity to wear ear plugs when working or ear phones with monitored listening.

3. Create a learning environment that is well organized and orderly.

4. Use calming and soothing colors for décor (pastels, neutrals).

5. Make sure transitions are well planned. Students will feel more secure knowing about changes in the schedule well in advance. All students benefit when the daily schedule offers the chance to slowly leave an unstructured activity such as recess and gradually enter into more and more structured activities. As students return from an unstructured activity (such as recess, fire drill, assembly), present a transition activity before beginning a formal task. Transitions are more successful when students can go from focused to unfocused activities, formal to informal and structured to unstructured. The most difficult times will be transitions from informal to formal activities, unfocused to focused, and unstructured to structured activities. The key is to examine your schedule and coordinate activities so they follow this pattern (Jones, 1994).

6. Offer the opportunity during the day for students to write thoughts in a journal, diary, or a computer notebook or to tape record thoughts.

7. Give your students plastic squeeze balls or balloons filled with sand or salt. These stress relievers provide something for busy fingers to touch when working during quiet times. They give a very active child the opportunity for tactile stimulus, which is necessary when they are trying to concentrate and work independently.

Sleep Patterns and the Brain

"Early to bed, early to rise, makes a man healthy, wealthy, and wise." This early inspirational verse may have more meaning than we ever knew! Studies looking further at the cortisol levels (stress inducing protein) in children found that those who went to bed earlier had less difficulty with stress levels. The pattern of early to bed seemed to provide healthier cortisol levels. Researcher Jeannie Brooks Gun noted that difficulties with cortisol levels affected blood and heart rates, weakened the immune system and made it harder to concentrate. As educators, we can only provide information about this research to parents in the hope that when they are more aware of how sleep affects the brain, they can encourage this change in personal lifestyle. For practical purposes, be aware of children who appear unduly tired, sleepy, or fatigued. When you observe this behavior, offer frequent breaks and provide time for them to get water. When you have a chance to speak to the child's parent or guardian, note this behavior and ask them to be aware of how sleep deprivation affects learning.

Good Nutrition

We rarely have the opportunity to influence our students' eating habits. They leave our care to go to the lunchroom, and we seldom have the occasion to see how much or what they eat. Other than arbitrary snacks at times during class, we may be unaware of their eating habits. However, the food a child consumes in the womb, during infancy, and as a toddler can have lasting effects on the child's habits and health. Be aware that health experts now agree that eating well can reduce the risk of **neural tube defects** such as spina bifida (a partially exposed spinal cord) and anencephaly (the near absence of a brain) (Williams, 2000). During the early 1990s, researchers found that these conditions occurred mainly in women who were low on folic acid, a B vitamin that abounds in green vegetables. The federal government now recommends that all women of childbearing age take 400 micrograms of folic acid daily and that pregnant women take 800. Oranges, spinach, cauliflower, and broccoli are a rich source of vitamin B (Williams, 2000).

Supplements

Can supplements boost brainpower? Reporters Karen Springen and T. Trent Gegan investigated that specific question in a recent *Newsweek* article. Here's what they found:

- *Ginkgo Biloba:* This highly touted memory aid comes from the leaves of an ornamental tree. It may help increase oxygen flow to the brain while acting as an antioxidant. One preliminary study suggests it may help relieve mild dementia. At the time of writing this book, there is no physical proof of this in research.

- *Vitamin E:* This antioxidant helps prevent heart disease and boost immune function. Preliminary studies suggest it may also slow the progression of Alzheimer's. No one has shown it can improve memory in healthy people.

- *DHEA:* After the age of 30, the adrenal glands produce less and less of this hormone. Mice given DHEA supplements excel on learning tasks. It's not clear whether people react in the same way.

- *Aspirin:* Regular use of nonsteroidal anti-inflammatories such as aspirin and ibuprofen may delay the onset of Alzheimer's. These drugs can cause gastrointestinal damage, but new versions may not.

- *Estrogen:* Besides lowering the risk of Alzheimer's disease in post-menopausal women, estrogen helps support normal brain function. Studies suggest that estrogen replacement therapy helps maintain both verbal and visual memory.

- *DHA:* This omega 3 fatty acid, abundant in breast milk, is critical for brain development in babies. No one has shown that it enhances cognition later in life, but supplements are popular.

Moods

When I taught middle school, I felt my student's moods were similar to the changing levels of a barometer. One day they would be friendly and talkative, the next day withdrawn and angry. My fellow middle school colleagues and I dismissed this changeable behavior as typical to middle school and blamed it on puberty. Today, research is just beginning to let us see for the first time the brain's emotional landscape and how the biochemistry of feelings can confuse the brain's pathways and affect its ability to think in a focused, clear manner. Dr. Marcus Raichle determined that moods could powerfully bias what people think, remember, and perceive. He has found that extreme emotions trigger heightened neural activity that appears to interfere with the brain's ability to process information. (Hotz, 2002a, p. A37).

As educators we often set the mood or tempo in our room by our actions. Therefore, it behooves us to follow the guidelines on the following page to avoid undue emotional stress:

- Treat all students with fairness. Avoid continually selecting one student or one gender over another.
- Provide fair and equal ways to select students for participation.
- Provide cool down interventions for class during unusually difficult times.
- Offer a firm but fair behavior program that offers equal numbers of reinforcements and incentives.
- Avoid sarcasm in any form.
- Never use abusive language, derogatory terms, or cultural put-downs.
- Maintain a positive, open-minded attitude.
- Provide second chances on an equal basis.
- Avoid comparisons and competition between students; develop teamwork rather than one against another situations.
- Avoid timed, repetitive drills based on solely competing with one another; instead, let students compete against their own personal bests.

Humor

The hippocampus and the amygdala are the brain structures involved in the process of our laughter, with the cerebral cortex relating the laughter and speech while bringing humor into the equation (Cardoso, 2000). In addition to helping interpret humor, the amygdala is very integral to facial recognition. The ability to recognize a face is essential to maintaining social reactions and relationships. John Ratey writes, "Being able to recognize faces is an important part of the human repertoire of social behaviors. For one thing, it is essential for survival, a key to determining whether a friend or a foe is approaching" (Ratey, 2001).

Here's a fun story from my past. My preschool special education class had just had a visit from a local police officer who did a wonderful job sharing information about the danger of strangers, learning to use 911, and the role of the police officer in the neighborhood. He titled his presentation "Danger, Stranger." My students were awed and inspired by his message. When he left I took the class for a break to the hallway where they stood in line for drinks at the fountain. As we stood waiting, a fellow colleague of mine whom I had not seen in some time walked by. I greeted him warmly with "Hello, stranger, where have you been hiding?" Behind me, came a loud scream, we both turned to my class to see a student with his arms up and back to the wall shouting, "Teacher, is that the stranger?" Both the amygdala and the hippocampus were working in tandem with emotions in this encounter!

Your day will have moments like these that you won't easily forget and that everyone can enjoy. Keep a small notebook on your desk just for sharing these private moments, funny thoughts, and silly experiences. On your "down days," grab this book and take it with you to lunch to remind yourself of the good things in your daily work life. Humor is healing and humor is helpful. Used in a positive way, humor can inspire all of us to feel less stressed and more positive about the daily grind. Laughter releases neurochemical transmitters called **endorphins**. These transmitters decrease indifference to pain and boost fortitude and enjoyable sensations. You do not need to be a Robin Williams, but showing respect for funny moments and adding a few of your own can lighten the spirits of your students and your colleagues.

Laughter used in the right place can be positive; laughter used in a rude or hurtful way can be quite damaging and spiteful. One colleague of mine had a student who was a regular class clown. Even my friend admitted this student was very humorous, and it was hard for the teacher not to laugh at his antics. My colleague was afraid that too much time was being spent in the class listening to this boy's humor. He wondered how to manage it and yet not stifle this boy's obvious talent. He asked for my suggestions, and I noted that I had handled a similar situation in my middle school classroom by talking with the "entertainer" privately. I spoke frankly to him about how much I enjoyed his humor but that it had to have its time and place. I offered him a time to perform on a regular basis for the class if he could control his comments all other times. It worked! My student looked forward to his time on stage, prepared for that, and actually got quite good at scripting his brief presentations. We all benefited. You may enhance humor, laughter, and good common fun by employing the brain breaks listed below:

Brain Breaks

- Have a "Riddle Day." Read riddle books, create riddles, and start a riddle chain where one person starts the riddle and another must finish it. Use large brown paper and markers to write a large class riddle.

- Read a funny chapter book to class and ask students to act out some of the events in the book.

- Allow certain times for jokes and funny stories to be told in class.

- Participate in theme days, such as "Math Day," "Music Day," or "Rainbow Day," where you and students dress up and decorate the room to reflect the topic.

- Teach magic tricks and have students perform the ones they know.

- Have students write or draw a picture about a funny happening, a joke, or an experience that made them laugh. Allow student volunteers to share their stories and pictures with the class.

- Provide puppets for students to use in creating stories and short performances for classmates.

- Have a "New Name Day." Let students select a new name for the day. Have each student wear a name tag that displays his or her new name. Everyone must try to remember and use the new name all day.

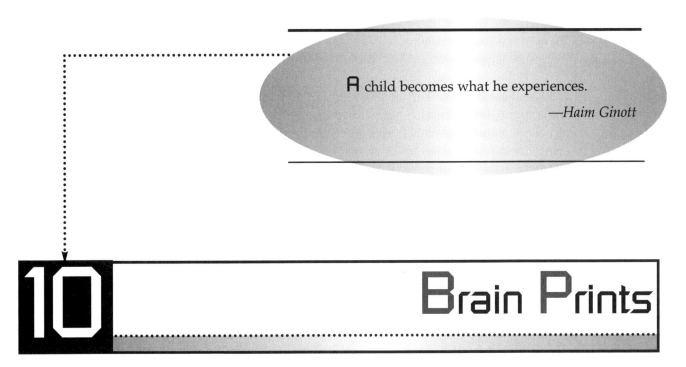

A child becomes what he experiences.

—*Haim Ginott*

10 Brain Prints

We know that every brain is exceptional and distinctive. Neuroscience is guiding us to the realization that the brain has its own predilection toward learning. Multiple factors, from genes to emotions, environment to experiences, stress to health, contribute to the developing, evolving brain. Brain research will continue to be at the leading edge of true educational change. It will also be at best exciting, defining, misleading, and contrary.

There continues to be great debate about the origins of intelligence. Some researchers' studies highlight the influence of the effects of genetics, others note family upbringing and still others share the influences of nutrition and behavior. Studies of twins focus on hereditary influences while some laboratory experiments are beginning to implicate the influence of environment. Nature and nurture are, without a doubt, interlinked. As educators and parents we must never lose sight of the critical and meaningful impact *we* have on learning and the personal development of the children in our care. Our impact is literally like putting "fingerprints on the brain" (Robertson, 2000). Therefore, we must remember that caregivers and parents working together can create successful modeling experiences that can offer opportunity and change for the developing child.

Parent/teacher communication is imperative in today's learning environment and will be critical to the student's follow-through and success. How can busy families and professionals stay on top of the learning experience? Create an avenue for communication by setting up a system for ongoing correspondence and recognition. This venue should be brief, positive, and to the point. It could be a brief message recorded on the class homework hotline about the daily plan or a web site devoted to your class. It might be a written note, printed form, or assignment notebook that goes home regularly. If you are using handwritten communication, select one distinctive color of paper for the form or notebook, so it stands out from all other documents going to the home. Keep the color consistent. Make the form simple to fill out and involve the child in doing so. Following is a typical form you might use. A student completes the form at the end of the day and the teacher

adds brief comments. The teacher also checks to see if the student's responses are appropriate to the daily situation. This form can be copied on a brightly-colored sheet of paper and clipped to a clipboard in the student's book bag for easy delivery and return.

To Home

Name _____

Circle one:

Monday	Tuesday	Wednesday	Thursday	Friday

Good start in morning	Yes	No
Cooperative behavior with teacher and students	Yes	No
On task in morning	Yes	No
On task in afternoon	Yes	No

Favorite activity today _____

I worked hardest on _____

Homework

Math	Yes	No	_____
Reading	Yes	No	_____
Language	Yes	No	_____
Other:	Yes	No	_____

Teacher agrees with above	Yes	No

Teacher comments _____

_____

_____

(Parents: Please complete the back of this sheet and return it.)

Figure 10-1: Sample Parent Communication Form

From Home

Name _____ Date _____

I read this form and discussed it with my child.

We tried different strategies
during homework time.   Yes   No

Information that is important to my child's learning environment _____

_____

_____

Here is something successful we have tried _____

_____

_____

Comments _____

_____

_____

_____

Signature_____

Figure 10-2: Sample Parent Reply Portion of Communication Form

---

Here are some other ways to get parents more involved in brain-based education:

- When you offer parent conference times or school-assigned parent meetings, present a learning styles inventory for parents to participate in so they can determine their own learning style.

- Encourage parents to see how the way they think and the way their child will respond to a learning task may be somewhat different.

- Create a phone tree or e-mail list for students and parents in your room so families can personally communicate with each other if they wish.

- Promote an open door policy for volunteering in the classroom.
- Let parents know you are encouraging their child's individuality by discovering their child's learning style and offering experiences based on that information.
- Set up a resource center where parents can borrow and share information about brain-based learning, articles, books, and videos.
- Send home the Web Sources page (page 151) for parents to explore.

If we are truly to be disciples of putting research into practice, then we know that studies indicate that immediate rehearsal and review are an integral part of learning information on a daily basis. In that spirit, this text concludes with a review of the principles that are critical in understanding brain-based theory.

In their book, *Mindshifts*, authors Caine, Caine, and Crowell (1994) urge us to recognize the principles of brain-based learning. They identify twelve areas in their text as critical to understanding our own brains and the way they work. These twelve areas, I believe, feature the general concepts of all brain-based learning theories that are represented within the context of this book. The authors' statements appear in boldface and my comments follow.

1. **The brain is a parallel processor.** Because the brain processes information in so many ways and through so many experiences, the educator needs to respond by encompassing many methods to respond to this brain variation.

2. **Learning engages the entire physiology.** Everything affects the functioning of the brain in learning. From nutrition to sleep, behaviors to beliefs, and daily habits — all of these factors are influencing the brain's growth.

3. **The search for meaning (making sense of our experience) and the consequential need to act on our environment is automatic.** The search for meaning is biological, and the learning environment needs to respond by offering the rituals, the variety, and the brevity necessary to make it all happen.

4. **The search for meaning takes place by "patterning."** (Note: The author's choice of the word patterning refers to the meaningful organization and categorization of information). This directs us as educators to help students create meaningful and personally-relevant patterns through themes, rituals, integration, and relevant life experiences.

5. **Emotions are critical and the heart of patterning.** The need for self-esteem, social interactions, personal biases, and perceptions must be considered as part of learning.

6. **The brain processes parts and wholes simultaneously.** Although left and

right hemispheres are significant, both hemispheres are intentionally working together. Education is parts and wholes — developmental and cumulative thoughts — and together they are conceptually interactive.

7. **Learning involves both focused attention and peripheral perception.** We learn within the structure and outside of the structure. Thus, the teacher must recognize all the factors that impact learning in the physical environment, including noise, temperature, visuals, scents, art, music, and activity.

8. **Learning always involves conscious and unconscious processes.** Our brain absorbs information constantly — some of which we are aware and some of which we have no conscious awareness of. We need to provide review, introspection of what we have done, memory techniques, exaggeration, and elaboration.

9. **The brain has different ways of organizing memory.** We need to respond by learning more about the memory and how to instruct students to develop theirs.

10. **We understand and remember best when facts and skills are embedded in our spatial memory.** Experience-based learning will benefit the student and offer immersion in a multitude of complex and interactive experiences. We take what they already know and build on it.

11. **The brain downshifts under perceived threats and learns optimally when appropriately challenged.** There is no place for humiliation, stress, and threat in an educational environment. We learn best in relaxed alertness.

12. **Each brain is unique.** Despite the same structural form, the circuitry is integrated differently in every brain. No two brains learn exactly the same way. We need to take personal strengths into consideration and offer experiences that are variable enough to attract individual interests.

As you work to implement brain-based learning into your classroom, keep focusing on ways to incorporate the fundamentals of this research into your instruction. Linking educational methodology and brain research is like matching a tie to a shirt or a sock to its mate. Once we understand the basic principles of the information we can integrate brain-based techniques into the curriculum to make this knowledge beneficial.

On the next page you will find a review of the brain-based guidelines that have been developed throughout this book

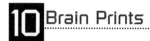

1. The information our brain absorbs is detected by our five senses. When we engage the senses, we engage learning. When we study sensory learning, we can determine an individual's learning style. Adapt your teaching to the student's learning style.

2. Our mood, emotional state, and condition of physical being all influence what we learn and for how long. If students are relaxed, secure, and feel positive about learning, they will be successful. Help their brains grow by providing a comfortable atmosphere for learning. Offer enrichment and exciting activities. Brevity, variety, and structure are keys to success.

3. Our brains reach certain milestones in their developing process, and we can engage the most rapid form of learning during these **critical prime times** of development.

4. Although the right and left sides of the brain work in tandem, most people have a favored hemisphere. The inclination for a side influences personal life choices, personality characteristics, skills, and learning styles throughout the life span. When learning, both sides function together.

5. Information is most likely to be placed into long-term recall if it makes sense and has meaning to the student. In short, feed the brain what it needs.

6. And finally, as an educator your role in this new millennium of the brain is to think of the following concrete directives when you consider your classroom and students:
   - Create an ever-changing, interactive learning environment.
   - Provide vigorous learning experiences.
   - Offer problem-solving opportunities.
   - Engage students in multiple learning activities.
   - Employ color coding.
   - Teach memory strategies.
   - Provide for the physical side of learning (exercise, stimulus, relaxation).
   - Enhance reinforcement.
   - Offer repetition with variety.
   - Stay up-to-date with new developments in brain research.
   - Provide support for transitions.
   - Link details to meaning.
   - Build on prior experience.
   - Believe in the positive.

The knowledge base we have now about the brain is just a starting point for what is to come. We can begin to dedicate ourselves to the wonderful and new practical implications for teaching based on the revolutionary brain research applications. We are in the process of discovering the success tools, which can develop the best in every student.

The field of brain-based learning is a very integral part of the future for all students and educators. It offers a positive way to begin to tailor learning to each and every individual we serve. Brain-based learning is our future and the future is now!

The Brain-Based Classroom	
What it is	**What it is NOT**
based on principles of neuroscience	traditional learning model
based on personal learning style	rote, sequential
built on prior learning experiences	built on isolated learning experience
designed with "whole" child in mind	designed to treat all children alike
ever-growing, ever-changing	same lesson plan every year
flexible, global, reflective	rigid, unyielding, firm
practices understanding of differences	punitive, humiliating
team driven	production driven

Figure 10-3: Characteristics of the Brain-Based Classroom

Abbott, M., Walton, C., Greenwood, C. (2002, March/April). Phonemic awareness in kindergarten and first grade. *Teaching Exceptional Children 34*(4), 20-25.

Amen, D. (1998). *Change your brain, change your life.* New York: Times Books/Random House.

Armstrong, T. (1998). *Awakening genius in the classroom.* Alexandria, VA: Association for Supervision and Curriculum Development.

Archer, A.& Gleason,M. (1989) *Skills for school success.* North Billerica MA: Curriculum Associates.

Barbe, W. Swassing, S. & Milone, C. (1977). *Teaching through modality strengths: concepts and practices.* Columbus,OH: Zaner Bloser, Inc.

Bandler, R. & Grinder, J. (1979). *Frogs into Princes.* Moab, UT: Real People Press.

Begley, S. (2000, Fall & Winter). Wired for thought. *Newsweek*, Special Issue, 25-32.

Bergonzi, C. (2000, Sept./Oct.). On the Brain. *The Walking Magazine 15*(6), 78-81.

Bronson, M. (1995). *The right stuff for children birth to 8.* Washington, D.C.: National Association for the Education of Young Children.

Brooks/Gunn, J. (2002, March 29). Going to bed early may help the kids better handle stress. *Arizona Republic*, E1.

Caine, G., Caine, R., & Crowell, S. (1994). *Mindshifts.* Tucson, AZ: Zephyr Press.

Cardoso, S. (2000). Our ancient laughing brain. *Cerebrum 2*(4), 15-20.

Cocke, A. (2002, Jan./Feb.). Brain may also pump up from workout. *Brain Work 12*(1).

Cowley, G & Underwood, A. (1998, June 15). Memory. *Newsweek*, 49-52.

Crenson, M., (2001, January 2). Rebels have cause; brain change. *The Arizona Republic*, E1 and E3.

Crowley, K,& Siegler, R. (1999, March/April). Explanation and generalization in young children's strategy learning. *Child Development 70*(2), 304-317.

Dennison, P., & Dennison, G. (1994). *Brain Gym (Teacher's ed., rev.).* Ventura, CA: Edu Kinesthetics.

Diamond M.,& Hopson, J. (1998). *Magic trees of the mind: How to nurture your child's intelligence, creativity and healthy emotions from birth through adolescence.* New York: Dutton.

Gardner, H. (1985). *Frames of mind: The theory of multiple intelligences.* New York: Basic Books.

Giedd, J. (2000, March/April). Is brain imaging useful in the diagnosis of Attention Deficit Hyperactivity Disorder? *Attention 6(4)*, 19.

Gopnik, G., Meltzoff, B., & Kuhl P. (1999). *The scientist in the crib.* Seattle, WA: University of Washington Press.

Guttman, M., (1997, May 18). Are you losing your mind? *USA Weekend*, 4-5.

Hanson, A. (2001). *Write brain write.* San Diego, CA: The Brain Store, Inc.

Holtz, R. (2000, December 17). Brain studies getting emotional response. *The Arizona Republic*, A37.

Horton K., Wilson. D., & Evans. M. (2001, July 30). Measuring automatic retrieval. *APA/Experimental Psychology, 57.*

Hotz, R. (2002, March 5). Left handers are found to have different brains. *Los Angeles Times*, A10.

Hotz, R. (2002, April 15). Toddler curiosity found to boost IQ. *Los Angeles Times*, A17.

Jacobs, W.J., and Nadel, L. (1985). Stress induced recovery of fears and phobias. *Psychological Review 92(4)*, 512-531.

Jensen, E. (1998). *Teaching with the brain in mind.* Alexandria, VA: Association for Supervision and Curriculum Development.

Jensen, E. (2000). *Brain based learning.* San Diego, CA: The Brain Store.

Jones, C.B. (1998). *Sourcebook on Attention Deficit Disorder (2nd Ed.).* San Antonio, TX: Communication Skill Builders.

Jones, C.B. (1994). *Attention Deficit Disorder: strategies for school age students.* San Antonio, TX: Communication Skill Builders.

Jones, C.B. (Ed.). (1999). *Parent articles on Attention Deficit/Hyperactivity Disorder.* San Antonio, TX. Communication Skill Builders.

Kaplan, P., Crawford S., & Nelson, S., (1977) *NICE: Nifty innovations for creative expression.* Denver, CO: Love Publishing Co.

Kilpatrick, J. (1995) Doing mathematics without understanding it. A commentary on Higbee and Kunihira. *Educational Psychologist 20(2)*, 65-68.

Kimura, D. (2002) A scientist dissents on sex and cognition. *Cerebellum 2(4)*, 69-84.

Koskovich, K. (1994). *Attention Deficit Disorder: strategies for school age students.* San Antonio, TX.

Levine, M. (1994). *Educational care.* Cambridge, MA: Educators Publishing Service, Inc.

Levitin, D. (2000, Fall). In search of the musical mind. *Cerebrum* 2(4), 31-49.

Lorayne, H. & Lucas, J. (1974). *The memory book.* New York: Ballantine Books.

Mastropieri & Scruggs, T. (1991). *Teaching students ways to remember.* Cambridge, MA: Brookline Press.

Michael, E., Keller, T., Carpenter, P. & Just, M. (2001). fMRI investigation of sentence comprehension by eye and by ear: modality fingerprints on cognitive processes. *Human Brain Mapping* 13(4), 239-252.

Patoine, B. (Ed.). (2001). *Staying sharp: the quality of life.* New York: The Dana Alliance for Brain Incentives and AARP Andrus Foundation.

Patoine, B. (Ed.). (2001). *Staying sharp: memory loss and aging.* New York: The Dana Alliance for Brain Incentives and AARP Andrus Foundation.

Payne, R. (1998). *A framework for understanding poverty.* Highlands, TX: RFT Publishing.

Pugh, K. (2001, September). Reading and the brain. *CEC (Council for Exceptional Children) Today 9*, 9.

Ratey, J. (2001). *A user's guide to the brain.* New York: Pantheon Books.

Restak, R. (2002). All in your head. *Modern Maturity* 45(1), 62-65.

Robertson, I. (2000). *Mind sculpture: unlocking your brain's untapped potential.* New York: Fromm.

Setley, M. (1995) *Taming the dragons.* St. Louis, MO: Starfish Publishing Company.

Schlegel, M. & Bos, C. (1994). In Jones, C. (Ed.), *Attention Deficit Disorder: strategies for school age students* (p. 129). San Antonio, TX: Communication Skill Builders.

Shimamira, A.P. (2000). The role of the prefrontal cortex in dynamic filtering. *Psychobiology 28*, 207-218.

Shore, R. (Ed.). (1997). *New insights into early development: rethinking the brain.* New York: Families and Work Institute.

Silver, H., Strong, R., & Perini, M. (2000). *So each may learn: integrating learning styles and multiple intelligence.* Baltimore, MD: Association for Supervision and Curriculum Development Publications.

Smith, F. (1986). *Insult to intelligence: the bureaucratic invasions of our classrooms.* Portsmouth, NH: Heinemann Educational Books.

References

Springen, K. & Gegan, T. T. (1998, June 15). Protecting your memory. *Newsweek*, 54.

Sousa, D.A. (2001). *How the brain learns (2nd Ed.)*. Thousand Oaks, CA: Corwin Press.

Sousa, D.A., (2001). *How the special needs brain learns*. Thousand Oaks, CA.: Corwin Press.

Sprenger, Marilee.B. (2002). *Becoming a "wiz" at brain based teaching*. Thousand Oaks, CA; Corwin Press.

Tomaino, C. (2002, March 31). When music heals body and soul. *Parade Magazine*, 5.

Vitale, B. (1982). *Unicorns are real: a right brained approach to learning*. Rolling Hills Estates, CA: Jaimar Press.

Weil, A. (2000). *Eating well for optimum health*. New York: Alfred A. Knopf.

Wichmann, F., Sharpe,L., & Gegenfurtner, K. (2002). The contributions of color to recognition memory for natural scenes. *Journal of Experimental Psychology* 28(3), 509-520.

Williams, S. (2000, Fall and Winter). The new face of nutrition." *Newsweek*, Special Edition, 42-45.

Wolfe, P. (2001, Fall) Opening the black box of the brain. *Books for Educators News* (Baltimore, MD: ASCD publications).

These web sites offer teachers information network on brain compatible learning (ideas and a chat room):
http://teachers.net/mailrings and **http://teachers.net/mentors/bcl**

This web site for the Families and Work Institute in New York offers their highly respected information on Rethinking the Brain:
http://www.familiesandwork.org

This is the web site for the American Association of Retired Persons, Andrus Foundation, which offers information on the aging brain:
http://www.andrus.org

This is the web site for The Dana Alliance for Brain Initiatives located in New York. They are a resource center for information on brain research:
http://www.dana.org

This web site describes itself as an effort to explore the fundamental nature of the brain and highlight applications that provide insights for this research:
http://www.brainresearch.com/

The web site for Corwin Press, Inc., which is a publisher of many books on brain-based strategies.
http://www.corwinpress.com

This web site shares information and research from the National Institute of Mental Health:
http://www.nimh.nih.gov

Association for Supervision and Curriculum Development site:
http://www.ascd.org

The author's web site where you can contact her directly:
http://www.clarejones.com

This is a web site where you can find numerous products, videos, and books about the brain:
http://www.brain.com

This is a web site for games, videos, books, and software about brain-based learning. There is also an excellent free newsletter available:
http://www.thebrainstore.com

This brain-based web site for parents and children offers games, advice, and resources:
http://www.funbrain.com

This web site has great information and materials. Of particular note is its section on neuroscience for kids.
http://www.neuroscience.com

Brain in the News
Dana Alliance for Brain Initiatives
5335 Wisconsin Ave., NW
Suite 440
Washington, DC 20015
www.dana.org

Brain Waves Newsletter
Editor
Minuteman Science Technology High School
758 Marrett Road
Lexington MA 02173 ($3/3issues/yr.)

Brain Based Newsletter
Dr. Joan Caulfield
Rockhurst College
1100 Rockhurst Road
Kansas City, Missouri 64110 ($15/3 issues/yr.)

Neuroscience Newsletter
1001 G. St. NW
Suite 1025
Washington, D. C.

The Harvard Brain Newsletter
Internet only: http://www.husn@hcs.harvard.edu.

Brain Waves Center (resource center on brain research), Tupelo Road, Bass River, MA 02664. www.brainwaves.com

The Brain Store (materials and books), 4202 Sorrento Valley Blvd. Suite B, San Diego California, 92121. 858-546-7555. www.thebrainstore.com

Earobics® Pro Plus (auditory training and phonics program), Don Johnston Inc., 1-800-999-4660, www.donjohnston.com

Expressions (software program that organizes thoughts and takes ideas from brainstorming to text outline), Sunburst Publications. Order directly from Sunburst at 1 800-786-3155

Fast Forward (phonics program for language impaired students), 300 Frank H. Ogawa Plaza, Suite 500, Oakland, CA. 94612-2040

Frameworks (commercially-made semantic webs and maps), Learning Disabilities Resources, P.O. Box 716, Bryn Mawr, PA. 19010, 1-800-869-8336

Inspiration (writing tool/software which helps students organize their thinking), published by Inspiration Software Company. Order at 1-800-637-0047 or www.edumatch.com/dctb

Journey into the Brain (software journey through the brain that features real pictures of human brains and neurons, for ages 6 to 11.), Morphonix software, 1-800-338-3844

Learning Styles Inventory (grades fourth to adult) published by Educational Activities. Order at 1-800-637-0047 from Special Times Warehouse or at www.edumatch.com/dctb

Learning Styles Inventory Assessment available for teacher use ($11.95) at www.howtolearn.com

Learning Styles Assessment, www.resourcesunlimited.com. For additional Learning Styles Inventories go to the Internet search site: www.google.com and enter "Learning Styles Inventory."

Memory Challenge! (Software game that improves visual memory skills, appropriate for all ages), Critical Thinking Software. Available through Special Times Catalog at 1-800-637-0047 or www.edumatch.com/dctb

Math Music Tapes (Addition, Subtraction, Multiplication, Division Raps), Pace Inc., 7803 Pickering, Kalamazoo, MI, 49002, 1-616-323-7940

Non-Carbonless notebook paper (NCR) Learning Disabilities Resources, P.O. Box 716, Bryn Mawr, and PA, 19010, 1-800-869-8336

Social skills training programs:
- Skill-Streaming for Preschool, the Elementary School Child and the Adolescent, Champaign, IL: Research Press, 1-800-519-2707, www.researchpress.com
- *Games to enhance Social and Emotional Skills: Sixty-six games that teach Children, Adolescents and Adults Skills Crucial to Success in Life.* Springfield, IL: Charles C. Thomas Publishing. Touch Math (multisensory math program to introduce basic computational skills), Innovative Learning Concepts, Inc., 6760, Corporate Drive, Colorado Springs, CO., 80919, 1-800-888 -9191, www.touchmath.com

Touch Math (multisensory program to introduce basic computational skills), Innovative Learning Concepts, Inc., 6760, Corporate Dr., Colorado Springs, CO, 80919, 1-800-888-9191, www.touchmath.com

Glossary

amygdala	the small, almond-shaped structure in the limbic area of the brain where your emotional memory lies
automatic memory	the conditioned response of your memory or the reflexive memory
axon	the long, string-like nerve fiber that is attached to a neuron. Its function is to pass on messages to other neurons.
BDNF	brain-derived neurotrophic protein that nourishes neurons and helps them maintain their health and regular function
brain stem	lower core of the brain; considered the most primitive part of the brain (often referred to as the reptilian brain,); where thoughts and information to the brain enter; monitors essential functions such as heartbeat and temperature
cerebellum	located at the base of the brain and believed to be the segment of the brain associated with balance, coordination, posture and various memories
cerebral cortex	the layer of cells that covers the cerebrum; thin but quite strong and contains all the neurons that are used for motor and cognitive processing
corpus callosum	the cluster of nerve fibers that acts like a rubber band connecting the left and right hemispheres of the brain
corticosteriods	chemical released into the bloodstream during stress; it interferes with the hippocampus and the processing of new information into memory; also referred to in the text as *cortisol*
declarative memory	another term for explicit long-term memory
dendrite	a thin, hair-like fiber that extends from the cell body of the neuron; receives impulses from other neurons
dopamine	a neurotransmitter involved in mood, behavior, and physical coordination
episodic memory	memory that involves location; is stored through the hippocampus
explicit memory	the conscious recall of information about people, objects, and places

frontal cortex	the top layer of cells covering the cerebrum that contains all of the neurons used for cognitive and motor processing
glial cell	brain cell that supports neurons
hippocampus	C-shaped structure involved with factual memory; it secretes some chemicals
implicit memory	the storage center of long-term memory that produces the unconscious recall of perceptual and motor skills
limbic system	a group of structures in the brain associated with memory and emotions
long-term memory	stores both conscious and non-conscious information
MRI	magnetic resonance imaging; a technique that uses a magnetic field to map brain structure
myelin	also called the *myelin sheath*; white fatty substance that covers the axons of most neurons; a substance that speeds the transmission of messages
neuron	the nerve cell of the brain involved in learning
neurotransmitters	chemicals that are produced in the neurons in order to transmit messages.
nondeclarative	another term used to describe implicit memory storage
PET scan	positron emission tomography; a brain imaging technique that maps the brain and can produce the images in color on a computer screen; uses radioactive glucose to measure the amount of glucose used by various sections of the brain
plasticity	the brain's ability to transform
phonemes	the units of sound in language, which when combined, make syllables
semantic memory	factual memory that is allied with the hippocampus.
serotonin	a chemical in the brain that controls aggressive behavior and helps with emotional control; offers a calming presence in the brain

short-term memory   part of brain where information is held momentarily

synapse   the tiny gap, which exists between the axon of a neuron and the dendrite of another one

thalamus   the structure in the limbic area of the brain that receives messages; where all sensory stimuli pass as it enters the brain with the exception of smell

19-04-98765432